insideMAN

insideMAN

Pioneering stories about
men and boys

Edited by Dan Bell & Glen Poole

Matador
9 Priory Business Park,
Wistow Road, Kibworth Beauchamp,
Leicestershire. LE8 0RX
Tel: 0116 279 2299
Email: books@troubador.co.uk
Web: www.troubador.co.uk/matador
Twitter: @matadorbooks

ISBN 978 1784625 337 PAPERBACK
ISBN 978 1784625 344 HARDBACK

British Library Cataloguing in Publication Data.
A catalogue record for this book is available from the British Library.

Typeset in 12pt Bembo by Troubador Publishing Ltd, Leicester, UK

Matador is an imprint of Troubador Publishing Ltd

This book is dedicated to all the great men and women who make it easier for the world to have conversations about men, manhood and masculinty.

Contents

Introduction

Not long ago we attended a meeting about men, such meetings are quite rare, but because we are known for speaking out on men's issues, we generally end up in more meetings about men and boys in a typical year than most people will in a lifetime. You see, when it comes to talking about men's issues, we are fortunate, as men in the country, to have a voice in the conversation about gender.

This particular meeting focused on how we could get more people talking about and addressing some of the social problems that have a disproportionate impact on men and boys – suicide, educational underachievement, shorter life expectancy, that type of thing.

Every man and woman in the room was committed to making a difference for men and boys and yet when one of us made the point that we needed to make sure that men's voices are heard, it didn't go down too well. The response went something like this:

'Ooh no, you can't say that, people will just think it's women who need a voice, because men already have all the power. If we say "men's voices need to be heard", people just won't listen to us.'

Yep, you heard right, this is how intelligent, well-intentioned people, who are genuinely committed to making a difference for men and boys think – they believe that if you, as a man, stand up and say that "men's voices need to be heard", people won't listen to you, so the best thing to do, as a man, is to keep quiet and not say what you really think.

And on one level we agree. If you attempt to enter the corridors of power, from the Houses of Parliament to your local council, no-one will listen to you if you try to make the case that "men's voices need to be heard". There may be more men "in power", but when it comes to gender issues, male and female politicians spend the majority of their time addressing the concerns of women and girls.

Is the appropriate response to this reality for men to stay quiet? We don't think so. If people in positions of power won't listen to men's voices, then the appropriate response is for more men to speak up about male suicide, men's health, boys' education, fatherlessness, fathers' rights, violence against men and boys and any other gender issue that concern us.

This is one reason why we launched *insideMAN* magazine in 2014, to make it easier for a diversity of men (and women) to talk about men, masculinity and manhood in the 21st century. And this book brings together some of our favourite articles from our first year, alongside exclusive content from some of the UK's leading thinkers on men's issues.

For too long men have been in the minority when it comes to conversations about gender. There are more than 7 billion people on the planet and every single one of us experiences life as a gendered human being. For the majority of adults this means either being a man or being a woman. Yet while one half of this equation is well served in the global conversation about gender, men and boys remain largely invisible.

This is not surprising when you consider the institutions that have been put in place to drive forward this important global conversation: the UN has an organisation dedicated to women, but not men; the European Union has a Women's Charter, but not a Men's Charter; the UK government has a Women's Minister, but no Men's Minister; universities across the land have courses in Women's Studies, but not Men's Studies; unions have women's officers, but not men's officers; our local and national newspapers have women's sections but not men's sections, and the list goes on and on.

And yet we know that men and boys all over the world have a gendered experience of life that is distinctly different from women and girls. On average we die younger, spend more time at work, are more likely to fail at school, are more likely to be the primary breadwinner for our family, are more likely to be separated from our children, are more likely to be victims of men's and women's violence, are more likely to be unemployed, imprisoned, homeless or addicted, and are more likely to die from suicide.

So how will publishing these articles solve this? Well in reality it won't. Each one of our articles for men and boys is a mere drop in the ocean of conversation about women and girls. And yet we know that drops can become ripples and ripples become waves, and so our intention is that these small conversations will have the potential to create big waves that in time will make a difference for men and boys.

We want to do everything we can to ensure the conversations generated by *insideMAN* are reflective of men and boys in all our diversity. We want to hear the voices of men from across the political spectrum; men of all sexualities, men of all nationalities, men and boys of all ages, men of all religions and beliefs, men of all physical and mental abilities and men with many different interests and experiences of life.

So if you feel that your voice – or the voice of a group of men or boys you are concerned about – isn't represented in this book, then please join the conversation. Write a blog, pitch an article, call a radio phone-in. We want to hear from men and boys of all backgrounds and for the sake of transparency there are three groups, who are generally excluded from discussions about gender, who we have tended to favour in this collection, and they are:

1. Men (as most people already speaking about gender are women, so the vast majority of articles we publish are written by men).

2. Non-feminists (because when it comes to gender politics most conversations about gender are viewed from a feminist perspective, so we welcome non-feminist writers into the conversation about gender).

3. People who focus on men's problems (as conversations about gender that include men, usually perpetuate the myth that "women HAVE problems and men ARE problems", which is why we welcome

people who focus on the "problems men have" into this discussion).

This doesn't mean that women, feminists and people concerned with "the problems that men cause" are not welcome to join the conversation. You are. In fact everyone is invited to take part in this important discussion, our only request has been that everyone expresses themselves in a way that ensures each other's voices can be heard.

Being heard is a two-way process. It involves speaking and listening – and for too long men and boys have either not spoken up about their experiences of being male, or have not been listened to when they do speak out. This book is a small but significant step towards giving men and boys in the UK a bigger voice in conversations about gender.

We hope you enjoy the book and get involved by encouraging others to buy a copy. You can do this by commenting, sharing some of the articles with friends and submitting your own ideas and articles if you want to. We can't promise to agree with everything you say, but we do promise we'll listen.

Finally, we'd like to offer our heartfelt thanks to everyone who contributed to the success of *insideMAN*'s first year. In particular, our thanks goes to all the writers who have so generously and freely provided articles for publication. Without them we wouldn't be having this important conversation about men and boys.

Dan and Glen

MEN AND MASCULINITY:

The invisible gender?

The Ancient Rules of Masculinity

By Martin Seager

Men have evolved alongside women and make up half of the human population. Humanity is gendered. Yet we still do not really think of men as having "gender issues". It somehow feels wrong to put it in those terms. As a society, we (both men and women) lack curiosity about what pressures and issues arise from being of the male gender. This may be partly because of a mythical belief that men are somehow doing OK and run the world anyway. Whilst some men are very powerful, however, the vast majority are not and powerful men are doing nothing in policy terms for their "brothers". There is still very little research into the psychology of being a man or a boy despite the fact that there are obvious gender differences in life expectancy, rates of suicide, addiction, crime, getting assaulted, homelessness and educational performance.

As a psychologist – and just as a human being who is trying to understand the human condition – I find this relative blindness to the male gender very striking. What is behind this silence about the gendered emotional worlds of men? Might the cause of the silence also explain the stark gender differences described above?

If we look around us it is not hard to find consistent evidence that there are ancient rules of masculinity that put pressure on men (and from an early age boys) to think, feel and behave in certain ways. These rules can still be seen in everyday life and in the stories that we tell ourselves in books, films, plays, TV shows and in popular culture. Myself and colleagues have hypothesised what these rules look like and we are beginning to research them to see if they can help to explain for example why men are less likely to seek help and more likely to go through with suicide.

These rules have already been "road tested" on various focus groups and found to have strong face validity. There are only three simple rules:

1. A real man is a fighter and a winner
2. A real man is a provider and a protector (of women, children and others)
3. A real man retains mastery and control

If we assume that these deep-seated "hero" rules are always acting upon men, then it helps to explain why men can feel such "masculine shame", for example, if they lose their job or need help or direction of any kind. These rules also fit with what we know about the evolution of the male as a fighter and hunter. The big question is whether these rules can change in a modern world or to what extent we have to help men find more modern ways of living up to them. For example, men can be given the message that they are *taking* control by seeking help, not *losing* control. Whatever else we do, we need to honour the male gender as having its own identity, needs and issues and we need to start designing our society to take account of the specific needs and differences relating to both genders.

Martin Seager is a Consultant Clinical Psychologist, mental health campaigner and activist, with a particular interest in men's issues and male psychology. Since 2006, he has been consultant to Central London Samaritans and was commissioned by the National Samaritans to write a review on the science of why talking helps and doesn't help people. Martin is a regular contributor to BBC radio broadcasts on mental health issues, and has authored many articles and chapters in various journals and books on many areas of mental health including men's issues.

Who Gets to Define what "Healthy" Masculinity is Anyway?

By Rick Belden

Over the last few years, I've seen more attempts than I can remember to define what constitutes appropriate and proper, often characterized as "healthy", manhood and masculinity. Some of these efforts are clear, grounded, and helpful. Some are well-intentioned but misguided and/or misinformed.

Others appear to be driven primarily by socio-political motivations, and in far too many cases, by an ongoing effort to demonize men, masculinity, and male power as inherently flawed, bad, evil, wrong and "toxic". Masculinity is seen as a source of problems and therefore must be restricted, restrained, and if possible, eliminated, with a corresponding retraining of men to rid them of their innately troublesome nature (e.g., the widespread "Teach men not to rape" meme).

One of the most prevalent and pervasive themes I've seen on this subject typically goes something like this:

Healthy masculinity is defined by how a man treats women.

This could not be more wrong. Healthy masculinity is defined, first and foremost, by the nature of a man's relationship with himself. He must know, understand, and be in conscious, ongoing relationship and dialog with:

- his wounds
- his history
- his needs
- his anger
- his sadness
- his grief
- his joy
- his strengths
- his weaknesses
- his purpose in life
- his shadow
- his power

A man's relationship to his own power is a critical element of a mature, healthy masculinity, and that relationship can be a tricky and difficult one for some men. The primal aspect of male power can be very intimidating, especially for men who spent their boyhoods with men who abused or avoided their own power. But true manhood is not possible without acceptance, application, and mastery of one's own power, in whatever forms are unique and appropriate for the individual.

Owning and applying one's power in a mature, healthy way carries with it the responsibility of owning the outcomes of doing so, both positive and negative. It also requires setting boundaries for what is and what is not within the scope of one's responsibility. A man must be willing to take responsibility for his own actions and inactions, his own successes and failures, without assuming responsibility for the actions, inactions, successes, and failures of others, however much he might feel pressured to do so.

Any man who defines himself primarily in terms of something external to himself (other people, objects, job, etc.) is in for a world of trouble. A man who regularly gives women's needs higher priority than his own is going to wind up very lost and very angry at some point in his life. He will then direct the effects of his suffering at himself, at those around him, or both.

A man will generally treat others, over the long term, only as well as he treats himself. A man who is in a healthy relationship with himself will treat others (women, children and animals as well as other men) with the same respect, consideration, and understanding he allows himself, and all of it will be coming from a place of authentic inner abundance rather than from a need to impress or meet external expectations.

It's hard for me to imagine the same folks who espouse the "healthy manhood is defined by how a man treats women" approach flipping the genders and saying "healthy womanhood is defined by how a woman treats men". Healthy relationships between men and women will not come by requiring one gender (male) to elevate the other (female) above itself. What we should be aiming for is parity and partnership. Telling boys and men that the number one priority in their lives should be the needs of girls and women takes all of us in the opposite direction.

The "healthy masculinity is defined by how a man treats women" approach essentially says that healthy, appropriate, mature masculine identity is to be determined on a performance basis by women, according to standards that would no doubt vary from time to time and woman to woman. This is a blueprint for confusion and frustration on the part of both men and women. Women cannot define masculinity for men, nor should they be expected to, any more than men can, or should be expected to, define the feminine for women.

The true source of healthy masculinity is within each man. It is waiting for him in his mind, his heart, and his body. It speaks to him in his dreams, his daydreams, and his fantasies. The pathways that can lead him to it are ancient and well-traveled by his ancestors. It is a journey that has been taken countless times over countless centuries, but it begins anew with the life of every newborn boy who enters this world.

Let's give each boy and each man the tools, the knowledge, the encouragement, and the freedom to take that journey in his own way, at his own pace. That is the one and only way that healthy masculinity will truly manifest and express itself in our world.

Rick Belden is an explorer and chronicler of the psychology and inner lives of men. His book, Iron Man Family Outing: Poems about Transition into a More Conscious Manhood, *is used by therapists, counsellors, and men's groups as an aid in the exploration of masculine psychology and men's issues, and as a resource for men who grew up in dysfunctional, abusive, or neglectful family systems.*

It's Time to Give Men a Break!

By Glen Poole

Men are everywhere. We're the politicians, the church leaders, the business owners and the sports stars.

Pick up a paper and the media's full of us – we're the murderers, the rapists, the scandal makers and the crooks.

Tune into a random radio phone-in and you'll soon find out what we think about football or politics.

You'll see us in the cinema; we're the goodies and the baddies in almost every major film – the protectors and the perpetrators, the cowards and the clowns.

With all the patriarchal power and privilege men are supposed to enjoy, why do I think that men need a break?

Well, we may always have a point of view about the world outside – and we may still occupy most of the senior positions in the outside world – but what's happening inside men?

Thirteen of us men will kill ourselves today, in the UK alone, and for each man who dies there will probably be an external factor we can point to, such as a divorce, drug addiction, debt or unemployment.

But what's happening inside the dozens of men who die from suicide each week, when the internal pain of living another day becomes greater than the fear of killing yourself?

And what's happening inside the rest of us men, those of us who aren't suicidal but still face challenges in life: the overweight, the unemployed, the lonely and the sick? The fathers struggling to connect with their kids, the partners in unhappy or abusive relationships, the stressed-out workers with not enough life in their work-life balance and the low-paid and unemployed men who face the emasculating shame of being a man who can't provide?

On the surface men have it all – the jobs, the money, the cars, the clothes, the power, the authority and the free time to play golf, watch football and laugh at Jeremy Clarkson. On the outside men are always acting out – drinking to excess, harassing women in the streets, grooming kids for sex and keeping the police and prison service busy.

But what's happening inside men?

From the day we are born, we are fed a story that there are only two types of men in the world. Men are either heroes or villains, we're either strong or weak and there is no shade or colour between the black or white choice of being a good man or a bad man.

What's it like for men, living within these narrow confines, between a heroic rock and a villainous hard place?

Take the daily onslaught of social media campaigns repeatedly telling the world how awful men are to women. How is the average man expected to respond?

We have two choices – pick a box – hero or villain.

Either we step into the protector role, like a good little man and speak out against the bad men ruining the world for our womenfolk – or we're a villain.

Men's expected role in the gender war – as in every

other war – is to choose a side; goodies or baddies. You either wear the "this is what a feminist looks like t-shirt" or you're a woman-hater; you either fight against the Germans or you're a cowardly traitor; you either support Emma Watson's #HeForShe campaign or you're a misogynist or a rape apologist.

What's it like for men to have such limited choices – and if men have all the power, why don't we just give ourselves more choice?

The sexist rallying cry of traditionalists has long been "women and children first"; for the liberal feminists, their sexist motto is "women and girls first". Can you see who's missing from both of those slogans? It's the invisible gender in both his forms – the good man and the bad man.

Who puts women and children first? It's the good man. Who do women and girls need protecting from? It's the bad man.

When William Hague was Foreign Secretary, he made an official announcement that "all men" should feel shame about war crimes against women – and to fail to do so was "unmanly". That's right male citizens – you're either a good man feeling shame or a bad "unmanly" man – pick a box.

So what's happening inside of the nation's men when we are repeatedly called upon to pick a box? Goodie or Baddie? Hero or Villain? Perpetrator or Protector?

The truth is, most of us are neither good nor bad. Most men are somewhere in the middle of the statistical bell curve that defines the male population.

Most men are not murderers, rapists, wife beaters or street harassers. Most men are not politicians, church leaders, business owners and sports stars. Most of us don't feel powerful and privileged. Thirteen of us will kill ourselves today. More of us will kill ourselves slowly with alcohol, cigarettes, drugs, poor diets, too much work and a lack of self-care.

What's happening to men on the inside?

Do men spend so much time focussed on what's on the outside – our job, our home, our bank balance, our football team, our political views – so we don't have to stop and listen to the constant internal pressure to prove ourselves to be a "good man" in the eyes of whoever it is we seek approval from today?

What would life be like if we didn't have to constantly prove our masculinity?

Statistically, most of us are fairly average. There's no shame in that. So what if we accepted that most men are already good enough?

We keep the country running; we generate wealth; we provide for our families; we take care of our kids; we contribute to our local communities and we make our friends' lives a little richer. Isn't that good enough?

It doesn't matter what gender you are, if you want to make a difference for men and boys, you can start by giving us average men a break!

Glen Poole is a leading expert on men's issues, UK co-ordinator for International Men's Day and author of the book Equality For Men. *He has established numerous grassroots projects for men and boys, is a regular media commentator and is news editor of* insideMAN *magazine.*

How Wearing Trousers went from a Symbol of Freedom, to a Straight-jacket for Masculinity

By Dr Arian Bloodwood

Joseph Van Aken, An English Family at Tea c.1720 © Tate Images

Look closely at the gentleman in the foreground of this picture. He's the head of this 1720s aristocratic household. He wears a wig, a dress, lacy underclothes, stockings and high heels – and there's no doubt he's a man.

Today it's almost unthinkable that men in public wear anything but trousers. This entirely arbitrary and very recent limitation on acceptable dress for men has implications that go deep into both the psyche of each individual, as well as into the very structure of democratic society.

When we wear clothes, the fabric drapes about our limbs, touches our skin, and gives us constant feedback about the position and attitude of our body. The garments we wear also need to bear on our bodies at specific points so that they stay in place and don't fall off: the shoulders and collar of a shirt, the waistband of trousers, the cuffs of a jacket, the snug fit of shoes. With these familiar areas of pressure and weight we develop an internal map of our body which is part of feeling 'at home' in our own body.

Finally, the structure of the garments themselves – the way the panels of fabric are cut and sewn into shapes – provide subtle pressures which suggest certain movements and restrict other movements.

So the experience of wearing clothing is like providing ourselves with a portable feedback loop which gives us a specific relationship with our body and offers a specific range of movements.

When we wear only trousers on our lower body, we experience our body in only one way and we tend to practice a limited range of movements. In effect when we wear the same garments all the time we affirm a cultural story that our male body has only a very limited capacity to feel and to express, and that our relationship with our body is simple and unvaried.

Of course wearing trousers doesn't actually prohibit us doing things like expressing affection or receiving touch. Rather, the body-level experience of being in trousers supports certain familiar and culturally acceptable ways to express ourselves – so that other forms of expression don't feel right and don't look right.

Beyond this personal experience, trousers are a symbol of social legitimacy and appropriate democratic participation. Trousers and democratic citizenship emerged at the same time. The Great Reform Act of 1832 was hailed at the time as a turning point in democratic participation, massively increasing the number of people able to vote. At the same time trousers and a simple military-style jacket, became *de rigueur* for men in public life. Trousers symbolised equality: the divide between the peasant in his smock and our 1720s aristocrat in his wig and silk stockings, was swept away by a garment available to all, elegant for all and practical for all.

Back then, trousers were an epochal step towards freedom and social participation. But now, nearly 200 years later, the cultural rejection of anything but trousers is

an appalling straightjacket. The 19th Century realisation that peasant and aristocrat are all the same under the skin, has become an oppressive trap for men as we intensely and minutely police each other to ensure we all appear the same and act the same. Variations from the norm are fiercely put down, emotionally through ridicule and humiliation, or physically through violence.

Wearing unfamiliar garments, like this Bloodwood skirtsuit from 2013, raise terrors at the intimate level of our relationship with our bodies. We are suddenly confronted with new possibilities of pleasures beyond our habitual patterns of proper 'masculine' body movements and flows of touch. It is common to experience 'gender vertigo' at this point – a dizzying questioning along the lines of: "If I enjoy this so much, does that mean I am gay/a woman/a transvestite?"

Alongside the personal level we are also confronted with the potential to be excluded from social participation at work, in our family, among friends and on the street. The fears arising at the level of our own bodies can be engaged through both growth work and play. But the fears around social exclusion have a very real basis; it is still not unheard of for men to be killed for transgressing gender norms.

But even when there is no risk of physical violence, inevitably people will be puzzled, and people who have power over you, like bosses or clients, may make decisions which disadvantage you. So it's helpful to have a simple verbal package to explain what you are doing and why it's important.

Moving beyond trousers moves us beyond trousers masculinity – the template of maleness of the last 200 years. Other garments are our license to explore our relationship with ourselves and our own body, and to explore other ways of engaging in social life beyond the restrictions on men's self-expression and interaction with others.

At the moment it's challenging for men to wear skirts and dresses on the street. But that's only because it's still very unusual. The best way to make it common is to claim it's perfectly legitimate and acceptable by simply doing it!

Dr Arian Bloodwood brings a unique perspective on masculinity through his wearing of "gender non-conforming" clothing since the 70s. Initially joining men's groups in Australia in the early 80s, he has been part of a wide range of approaches to men's issues, including experiential workshops, ritual work, political activism, and a PhD in men and progressive change. His driving theme is the massive opportunities for men to step beyond gender to enrich their lives and create new selves. He currently lives in London where he offers a spiritually-oriented accounting service. Visit his website www.bloodwood.org

The Gaslighting of Modern Masculinity

By Karen Woodall

I am a therapist working at the coalface of family separation. I get to see the reality of what men and women go through when the family fractures. I have also been involved in policy development around family separation with the UK government. I know from this experience that mothers and fathers are not equal when they face family separation.

I work in the messy places where men, women and children are wounded and raw from loss and life change. Instead of being helped by emotional paramedics however, the adults are surrounded by legal vampires and individual rights based services, who feed from the wreckage of the broken relationship. Children on the other hand are mostly just overlooked.

Mothers however, have at least the gender neutral laws and their gendered application to support them. The Children Act 1989 governs the world of the separated family along with various regulations about child maintenance. These laws, neutral in that they cover parents generically, are applied in a gendered manner by family services who are mostly steeped in the notion of mother as carer and father as provider. Motherhood is therefore upheld and seen as vital, whilst what it means to be human and necessary in a child's life, for men as fathers, is slowly dimmed by those who circle the family.

A man who faces the breakdown of his family faces the gas-lighting of his masculinity as he is relentlessly persuaded into the acceptance of his unnecessary role in his children's lives. Absent fathers are all, in popular consciousness, 'deadbeat dads' because the institutionalised terrorism faced by fathers in the months and years after separation is hidden from public view. The eradication of male authority, the shaming of men through domestic violence perpetrator programmes and the forced supervision of their 'contact' relationship with their children, force men along a conveyor built towards acceptance of their pointlessness in their child's life. At the end of which a man is either grateful for the time he is 'allowed' with his child and is obedient or he is deemed unworthy and rejected by the system.

Gas-lighting the masculine is based upon the notion that heterosexual men are dangerous to women and therefore to children. It is born of the political ideology of feminism and the architects who wrote 'it cannot be assumed that men are bound to be an asset to family life or that the presence of fathers in families is necessarily a means to social cohesion'. (1) Thus, a man who seeks to continue his relationship with his children after separation in full possession of his masculinity is doomed unless the mother of his children is accepting of that, because gas-lighting of the masculine is an institutionalised part of the family court process.

When I meet separated fathers who are losing their children and their own selves to this process, it feels as if I am meeting the ghosts of men who once were but who are no longer in full possession of their masculinity. Broken, frightened, unable to know their own mind. Questioning their very existence, these men are stripped of dignity, hope and connection to their children. My first task in supporting these dads, is to breathe life back into their masculinity and turn up the gaslight so that they can see themselves in the reflection of a healing mirror. This gives back what has been stolen by the institutionalised shaming and restores belief that as fathers they deserve to be helped and heard.

Down in the darkest places however, this institutionalised gas-lighting of fathers continues. Denied, dismissed and diminished in the outside world, this is what every man, in every family, in every town in this land will face should he find himself in the badlands of family separation. Crafted by the hands of women, family policy is designed to minimise the role of father and venerate the role of mother and gas-lighting men is how this is achieved. It begins when the family separates and ends when dad is dead and gone, either literally or figuratively. And on the surface of our world, those who know and speak about it are ridiculed and those who suffer it are reduced to shadows haunting the spaces in a child's life where a father used to be.

Karen Woodall is writer, researcher and practitioner working with families affected by Parental Alienation. She works at the Family Separation Clinic where she and her colleagues develop treatment routes for families affected by the problem. Karen describes herself as a "recovering feminist" and is a fierce critic of current approaches to handling family separation and attracts a passionate international following at her personal blog: www.karenwoodall.wordpress.com

(1) Patricia Hewitt, Anna Coote and Harriet Harman in the IPPR briefing 'The Family Way' – 1990

Crisis? What Crisis?

By Mark Simpson

The 'crisis of masculinity' is a phrase you read a lot these days in the media. Because we all love a good crisis it has become a hairy cliché of our times, one regularly proffered by pundits and politicians to grab our attention.

As a measure of how emptied of meaning the phrase has become, the outdoor cabaret artist Bear Grylls used it recently to promote an unreality TV show which dumped a random group of men on a tropical island with no potable water and no X Boxes. The old Etonian and Chief Scout claimed the show would be, in an age when 'masculinity was in crisis', a 'real test of what it means to be a man'. Because masculinity – unlike femininity – is timeless and unchanging, and about skid marks and killing your lunch with your bare hands. On primetime.

I don't believe in a crisis of masculinity. Or rather, I believe people who talk about a crisis of masculinity are usually talking about their own – about masculinity not being what they think or expect it should be.

I think it's great that masculinity is being talked about these days. That it's no longer something that is taken for granted. That it has become self-conscious. But that's not a crisis. That's a liberation – from assumptions. Which in turn represents a massive opportunity of possibilities for men. Which is something to celebrate not wring your hands over.

Once upon a not so distant time, back in the late 20th Century when I was growing up, masculinity wasn't in crisis. It was doing just fine, unfortunately. We all knew what masculinity was. Or rather, we knew what it *wasn't*. What masculinity wasn't was very, very important. As a man, your balls depended on it.

It wasn't sensual or sensitive. It wasn't colourful. It wasn't passive. And it certainly wasn't gay. Masculinity was uniformity – and difference was queer. And queerness of course was emasculation.

Likewise the male body was largely an instrumental thing – for extracting coal, building ships, bringing home the bacon, accumulating capital, fighting wars, sinking pints, scoring goals, making babies and putting the rubbish out. And not bloody whingeing about it.

Of course, this cartoonish code doesn't describe how men actually were, or lived their lives. But these were the rules that everyone knew. You broke them at your peril – so of course many post-war youth cults did just that, flagrantly: Mods, glam rockers, punks and New Romantics all rebelled, gorgeously, against that dreary code and really wound their dads up – which was a major reason why many of them did it.

But the Victorian-Edwardian world of industrialism and imperialism, along with the sexual division of labour it was based on, that dominated much the 20th Century and (re)produced that code has largely gone. Hence those unfunny, usually American, 'man code' books of prissy 'do's and (mostly) don'ts' that were popular a few years back – that mostly seemed to revolve around anxiety about urinals. Once you have to spell it out like that it's so over, baby.

American urinal anxiety aside, gay legal equality and widespread acceptance (in the UK) today is further proof that the epoch that criminalised Wilde and Turing – and which policed all men's behaviour with homophobia – is mostly in the past. And now that the fear of queerness isn't what it used to be, men in general are free to do and be and try and feel all kinds of things that were completely *verboten* before. Even touching and kissing their mates when their football team hasn't scored and they haven't drunk ten pints.

But perhaps the most obvious and eye-catching example of how the 'crisis of masculinity' has in fact been a liberation is what has happened to the male body. No longer an instrumental thing labouring in darkness, it has been radically redesigned to give and especially receive pleasure, and possibly a light fingering. It has become an adult bouncy castle.

Everywhere you look, billboards, telly, movies, the bus stop, you can see scantily-dressed young men 'inviting the gaze'. The 'passive' narcissistic pleasure of being looked at once considered *the* feminine quality has become something that selfie-admiring young men today have eagerly embraced.

In his 1972 classic *Ways of Seeing*, the art critic John Berger famously stated: 'Men act and women appear. Men look at women. Women watch themselves being looked at.' That formula, which seemed to describe the world so well for so many decades, is definitely 'in crisis'. As well as acting, men are doing an awful lot of appearing nowadays.

And I for one am very happy to finally see them.

Mark Simpson is an English author and journalist who is credited/blamed for coining the term "metrosexual" and who has also been described as the world's most perceptive and witty writer about masculinity. Mark is author of several acclaimed books, including Male Impersonators *and* Saint Morrissey. *You can read his writing on his blog www. marksimpson.com and follow him on Twitter @ marksimpsonist*

MEN
IN SOCIETY:

Tom, Dick and Harry

Is Finding Equality just as Difficult for Boys in the Current Climate?

By Shane Ryan

Working for an organisation set up to help our boys and young men seems to elicit the strangest of responses. People often make assumptions about our purpose. They may think we are fanatical about men's rights or are pushing a "pro-male" agenda. If we mention the m-word, "masculinity", they expect special pleading about how hard all men and boys have it, regardless of male privilege.

Such sceptics are often amazed when they get a closer look at our evidence based work supporting boys and young men in less affluent areas in living the life they aspire to and making a positive contribution to their own future and to the community.

I point out to those who are suspicious of an organisation set up specifically to help young men that this is the other side of the equation to all the great work being done to empower our young women. We understand that work is crucial and we believe ours is just as vital particularly with many young men searching for a sense of purpose and significance in wider society.

I have two boys and two girls and it was the experience of being the father of a young woman first which led me to observe how we sometimes view young men. I am very proud of my oldest daughter, a quick-witted 28-year-old, never afraid to help others or speak out against injustice. I remember the changing reactions the outside world had to her as she became a teenager. Fathers will know what I mean. Walking down the street, I noticed that where once men used to smile at her, now they looked her up and down, or just plain stared. It is a look I understand only too well and I felt very protective.

But what I didn't expect was that I would experience just as strong a reaction as my boys became teenagers. As far as the outside world is concerned, they seemed to have changed. But unlike my daughter, the perception seems to be that they're now a threat.

As they grow beyond six foot, the looks they attract are generally a mix of fear and apprehension even on the local streets where they grew up. Sometimes it's aggression. Yet these are two studious and well-mannered young men still young enough to think it is fun to play pass the parcel along with their 4-year-old sister.

We have to think carefully about the messages we are sending to young men. If we show them that we only think negatively about them, we risk alienating them at just the time when they face the pressures of growing up. Our charity works with hundreds of young men and we see how vulnerable they are to being corralled into a direction they don't want to go. In a society which already thinks they are a problem and seeks to deal with them in a punitive manner, they can become scared and frustrated in the search for who they should be and where they fit in.

Some might say this is part of growing up. But unfortunately coping alone with these emotional pressures can come out as aggression. And they often feel threatened themselves.

A study we conducted with young men across nine London boroughs after the 2011 disturbances found that the two things they fear most are the police and other young men of their own age – has much changed? I ask this at a time where according to the last Crime Survey for England and Wales young men are still most likely to be the victims of violent crime across the UK, and where according to recent research by the Institute for Fiscal Studies, men and young people are hit hardest by the shrinking of wages following the financial crisis.

And, alarmingly, boys under ten are nearly twice as likely to suffer from mental health disorders as girls and boys are still three times more likely to be permanently excluded from school. That makes it no surprise that amongst the young, 78% of suicides are male.

At the end of 2014, a new study containing research carried out by the Nuffield Foundation in the UK showed that 1 in 3 young people affected by child sexual exploitation were male. Follow-up interviews by NatCen Social Research with professionals who work with these children, like teachers, health workers and youth offending teams, found that these professionals can be less protective of boys than girls. That means they can miss key points for potential intervention which can be critical for these children.

If we demonize boys, or fail to protect them we

miss a valuable opportunity to encourage them to choose a well-informed path into adolescence. Telling boys to "man up" sends them the wrong message especially when it is usually used as an indication that they need to be tougher. It not only encourages them to feel they need to skip childhood and become a man quickly, but also be ready to use force to defend themselves and detach themselves from what they are feeling. This risks pushing them into alliances with people who are known for being able to "take care of themselves" and even to extremist views and actions (in some cases), as they search for a sense of purpose and belonging.

We talk constantly about role models as if they are the answer to all our problems but that approach by itself is a cop-out. It allows us to shirk our shared responsibility to boys and young men in general. We also allow ourselves to be seduced by the idea of inner city gangs, when constant tales of gang warfare just feed the idea of young men in particular as violent and out of control. The real hidden issues here are poverty, discrimination and generations of young men without some of the historical routes to opportunity, self-efficacy and self-worth. Change starts with acknowledging that providing targeted help for young men and considering the facts at hand is the right thing to do morally, socially and even economically.

As I look at my own boys playing party games with their sister on her birthday, I am reminded that they are still just children. We need to try to protect that childhood for all children particularly from impoverished backgrounds whatever their gender. We have to realise that it is "OK" to look after our boys too and help them on their journey in becoming our future men. They need us.

Shane Ryan is a writer and Chief Executive of the charity Working With Men. Working With Men have built a national reputation as a solution-focused organisation, offering multi-award winning evidence based approaches to community challenges and issues particularly around conflict and transition, father's development, masculinity, youth unemployment and men's health. Shane is the Chair of the Aire Centre, Vice Chair of Children England a fellow of the Royal Society of Arts and has over 25 years' experience working with young people.

The Problem with Leaving Boys Out of the Results Day Picture

By Dan Bell

Each August the publication of the year's A Level results are accompanied by the inevitable rash of Front Page Leaping Blondes™.

The fact that newspaper photographers are so skilled at seeking out A Level and GCSE students who are also pretty, middle-class girls, is now such a cliché that articles like this one are published about it almost as often as the pictures themselves.

These articles tend to argue that FPLBs™ are another example of our society's objectification of women – girls prized for their looks not their brains.

There's obviously some truth to this – where are all the less attractive girls? And for that matter, where are all the black and Asian girls? Don't they do well in exams too?

But this is a selective analysis both of who's missing from the front pages on results day and why it's a problem. The primary omission isn't unattractive girls, or girls from minority backgrounds. It's boys.

And it's also boys who really are missing out on educational achievement. In January 2014, UCAS reported that over a third more girls were applying for university than boys, leading the head of the organisation to state boys were becoming "a disadvantaged group".

When the year's results came in, it turned out the gap had widened even further.

What does it say then, if "a disadvantaged group" is consistently left out of the images that show who is and can be successful? Results day pictures that only show pretty girls may objectify women, but they also tell boys academic success isn't for them in the first place.

And this comes in context of other images of young men that are pervasive. A 2009 media analysis of news reports found depictions of teenage boys were overwhelmingly negative - with young men most likely to be portrayed in a positive light if they had died.

Meanwhile, recent high-profile anti-sexism campaigns now routinely portray the young men who do get into university as misogynists and sexual predators.

But all of this, including the pictures of FPLBs™, may in fact be a manifestation of something boys have already been told from a very young age indeed.

A 2010 study of boys in primary schools – with the sinister title of 'Gender Expectations and Stereotype Threat' – suggested that under-performance among boys in most national exams could be linked to adults' lower expectations of them.

Bonny Hartley, the study's lead author, told the *Daily Mail*: "By seven or eight years old, children of both genders believe that boys are less focused, able, and successful than girls – and think that adults endorse this stereotype. There are signs that these expectations have the potential to become self-fulfilling in influencing children's actual conduct and achievement."

Her study found that girls as young as four think they are cleverer, try harder and are better behaved than equivalent boys. By the age of seven and eight, boys agreed with them.

The study was reflected in the findings of a 2012 report by the All Party Parliamentary Group on Literacy, which found reading was not seen as a "masculine thing" by boys – leaving them lagging behind girls from the age of four. It found boys are held back by a "number of gender stereotypes which seem to kick in early".

None of this should come as much of a surprise. It is now widely accepted that if you consistently have low expectations of a certain group, those expectations tend to become a self-fulfilling prophecy. The puzzling thing is why this awareness is so rarely applied to underachievement among boys.

By all means be concerned about the objectification of female students in the results day newspapers. But you should also be just as concerned about the boys who aren't there at all.

Dan Bell is an award-winning journalist who has written for national news outlets both in the US and the UK, including the BBC, The Guardian *and* ITN. *He is Features Editor of* insideMAN *magazine.*

What do Urinals Tell us About a Man's Right to Bodily Integrity?

By Damien Ridge

Men are curious about what other blokes have, but are conscious not to be caught out. My brother told me about a heterosexual friend who – while, standing at a urinal – tried to turn his head stealthily to the left to get a sneaky peek at his neighbour. But he ended up accidentally splashing another man standing next to him.

However, men and their behaviours are increasingly drawing the ire of the public, not amusement. Only recently, a German court had to step in to uphold the right of men to urinate while standing, regardless of their poor aiming techniques. Men are also annoying the public in other ways, like taking up too much space with their "classic legs splayed" position on public transport.

I acknowledge the annoyance that some of you might have with men. But what I do find interesting in all the irritation directed at the male sex is the shrinking space available for men to just be themselves. Ironically, "all-powerful" men have become objectified, and we are little interested in hearing about how they feel about all this. Intriguingly, the metaphors around urinals are instructive here.

An influential sociologist, Erving Goffman, believed

that what we could deduce from the way that public toilets were stylised is that women were supposed to have lovelier surroundings for the elimination of their waste products and nice places to interact with other women away from the gaze of men and in order to attend to their appearances (1).

Public toilet facilities for men, on the other hand, were frequently paired down, often to just a urinal. A kind of assembly line for the production of urine if you like. Goffman believed that while the gents and ladies were thought of as just the natural order of things, they were actually crucial in producing some of the differences we see in men and women.

Inspired by the famous on-street urinals of Paris beginning in the mid-19th Century, the *vespasiennes* or *pissoirs*, many street urinals in London now don't have any privacy at all. All the world's a stage when men stand and urinate, literally. Society long ago decided that men do not have the same rights to privacy as women. This can create trauma for awkward male adolescents, for instance, forced to shower with other boys in shared showers.

Unease around men and their urine as a kind of "filth", and the need to protect women from unruly men has a lingering history (2). But our subconscious anxieties burst into the public consciousness with Duchamp's invention of conceptual art, via the Fountain in 1917. The Fountain was basically a sideways urinal, as some people pointed out at the time. But brilliantly, the Fountain scandalised a whole generation, bringing to the surface our fears around men, urine and their sexuality.

Urinals literally became a battleground, with heteronormativity being one crusade (i.e. the idea heterosexual practices should be promoted as natural). Before Grindr, when homosexuality was criminalised, men took to urinals as a semi-private space to find other partners. Urinals – and their ambiguity – provided an excellent way for men "in the know" to meet other men. The outcomes of authorities pushing homosexual men to the fringes of society were annoying to those same authorities, who subsequently passed criminal laws targeting such loitering men (3).

Today, the Internet and social media are the main combat zones. For instance, there is the YouTube clip that did the rounds last year, shaming men for harassing a beautiful young woman walking around New York – 100 incidents in 10 hours – as the producers of the clip claimed. But less publicised was the level of harassment that an athletic young man received for doing the New York walk around – 30 incidents of harassment claimed in three hours – including from many women.

So men are the disposable repositories of our (somewhat sexualized) anxieties. It is okay to objectify men so that we can discuss "the problem". For instance, we rightly care about female genital mutilation, but rubbish those concerned about the genital mutilation of infant boys. Thus a recent editorial in London's *Evening Standard* effectively denied any space for male suffering by advocating for "boys to get behind the campaign to end female genital mutilation". To say that infant boys should not have parts of their genitals removed is weirdly unpopular.

We want to encourage men to tell us how they feel on the one hand. However, we live in a world where men's feelings about key issues of interest to them are mocked or go unheard. The trouble is, we don't yet have a word for this mixed message we give to men, this cold-shoulder treatment. Could it be to engage in "man blanking"?

Damien Ridge is Professor of Health Studies at the University of Westminster. He has published over 50 academic papers in leading journals, and a book on how people actually set about recovering from depression (Jessica Kingsley Publishers, 2009). Damien has broad research interests in health, leading research into the patient experience, mental health, HIV, chronic pain, health services, masculinity and men's wellbeing.

---

(1) Goffman, E., The arrangement between the sexes. *Theory and Society*, 1977. 4(3): p. 301-331.

(2) Cooper, A., et al., Rooms of Their Own: Public toilets and gendered citizens in a New Zealand city, 1860-1940. *Gender, Place & Culture*, 2000. 7(4): p. 417-433.

(3) Johnson, P., Ordinary folk and Cottaging: Law, Morality, and Public Sex. *Journal of Law and Society*, 2007. 34(4): p. 520-43.

Thoughts on Being a Gay Christian Man

By Robin Fox

I'm writing this as a Methodist minister who happens to be gay. In many ways I find myself one of the most unlikely gay rights activists ever.

Well, perhaps "Activist" is too strong a word – I'm certainly not one of the "Loud and Proud" brigade, but to me, this is an area of justice where I believe I can't remain quiet.

I did not choose to be attracted to men rather than women. I accept that the jury is still out (if you'll pardon the expression) as to what causes homosexuality, but in the same way as people do not choose the colour of their skin or hair, or which hand they write with, so orientation is not a choice. If you are heterosexual, has anyone asked you why you are attracted to the opposite sex, or why you chose to be straight?

I believe that on the whole, pastorally speaking, the church's attitude to LGBT people has been a disaster. Of course there are exceptions to the rule, some wonderful exceptions, and I believe that there has been the beginnings of a significant change in recent years, but on the whole, it leaves a lot to be desired.

Having said that, whilst the beliefs that people have are still as strong as ever, I believe that we are getting somewhere – it seems to me that recently there has been a change in the tone of the debate, and perhaps people are starting to listen to each other?

Or perhaps it's that aside from the usual "clobber texts" of the Bible (Sodom and Gomorrah, Leviticus 18:22, Romans 1 and others), people are starting to remember that Jesus said that the first and greatest commandment is to love the Lord your God, and the second is to love your neighbour as yourself (Matthew 22:37 – 40).

If all the law and prophets hang on these commandments of Jesus, can we please see more evidence of "Love your neighbour" in the tone of future debates?

So, should the church permit same-sex marriage? I believe that yes, it should. Many Christians believe the Church of England and the Church in Wales are prevented by the teachings of the bible from doing so, and so far, only the Quakers and Unitarians have "opted in" to allow this. I find it sad that given how quick people are to say that there is a broad spectrum of beliefs on this matter, the practice in all the mainstream denominations only caters for one side of that spectrum.

Now do not get me wrong, I am not advocating "Anything goes". The example of the gay Methodist minister Paul Flowers, who was suspended from the Church after admitting to drugs charges, has shown what can happen when things get out of control, and the church does need to be a voice against the anything goes attitude of society, (that really was not a good time in which to be a gay Methodist minister). But to me, two people of the same sex who love each other, who also love God and want to express that love by wishing to be married in church, is hardly anything goes.

Disagree with me if you like, all I ask is that you keep it civil. I'm always happy to discuss this in more depth. No serious question is off the table. If we disagree but can still have a sensible chat over a coffee or something stronger, I can live with that.

White Male Football Fans: The Scum it's Great to Hate

By Martin Daubney

One cold Saturday night in 1989, in my home town of Nottingham, I witnessed first hand one of the most harrowing scenes of my life, when I saw a football fan bludgeoned to near-death.

A pack of 15-odd brawling geezers – 'home' Nottingham Forest fans and visiting Aston Villa – erupted from a nearby bar in a shower of smashing glass, beer and expletives, and I instinctively stepped back into a shop doorway just yards from the grisly scene.

Severely outnumbered by Forest, the away fans quickly scarpered, leaving one isolated figure in a Villa shirt. They swarmed on him like rats, dragging him to the floor, where they repeatedly stamped on him, with one even kneeling and glassing his head in a frenzy.

The bloodied, unconscious man's life was only saved, I think, by a woman, who bravely stepped in, screaming for mercy, sending the Forest fans fleeing, one of whom ran past me, his features displaying a primal rage I'll never forget. This was humanity at its very, very ugliest.

The incident deeply troubled me, and over the following weeks I scoured the local and national press, hoping to discover what had become of that poor Villa fan, whom I feared may be dead, yet hoped was not. But, even locally, the story never even made a single column inch.

My heavy-hearted conclusion, as a working-class Forest fan myself was, "It's just white, pissed-up, working-class football scum trying to kill each other on a Saturday night. Where's the story in that?"

So while the two events are seemingly connected only by football, my own recollections – and the media's indifference to it – made the mass spewing of righteous indignation in response to a story in early 2015 about "Chelsea racists" on the Paris Metro hard to fathom.

Let's agree: those Chelsea fans are bigoted morons and racism has no place in today's corporate-friendly game, just like a Villa fan being kicked into a likely coma has no place either. But most level-headed football fans saw this for what it was: a few meatheads that in no way represent the vast majority of decent fans. They'll get banned and we'll quickly move on, we thought.

But no. What followed was a thoroughly modern, social-media-driven and utterly predictable game of Top Trumps: "I'm More Offended Than You" Edition. David Cameron said the incident was "extremely disturbing and very worrying". Nick Clegg raised him, declaring it "grotesque" while the UN, better equipped to comment on the Islamic State's butchery in Syria than a footballing matter, called it "cruel".

Of course, the most indignant response came from the army of snobs and mobs on the internet. Within hours of the Metro footage breaking on *Sky News*, it emerged one of the protagonists, Josh Parsons, had previously posed for a selfie with Nigel Farage. The snobs, champagne socialists and Guardianistas went into a state of near-orgasmic piety: this was all the "proof" they needed that all white, working-class football fans are intrinsically racist.

There have now been 35 articles on the *Guardian* website micro-analysing the incident, underpinned by thousands of outraged comments, that has earned not just the Chelsea racists but white, working-class, male football fans in general the label "vermin". These articles argue such "thugs" bring "shame to our entire nation" – and all on a website where any slight criticism of Muslims, women, people who are of colour, gay or transgender is moderated out of existence.

Just as previously the Dapper Laughs and Julien Blanc incidents were "proof" that all white, working-class "lads" are misogynistic rape apologists, the Chelsea racism incident perfectly fitted another of their pre-ordained, quasi-feminist narratives: "Britain is going to hell – and white, working-class men are to blame!"

From the same quarter that has opined itself dry on the mantra "ISIS is in no way representative of Islam" a typically misguided *Guardian* comment was that "this virulent hatred, spite and vicious antagonism seems to be the norm for football crowds". The commenter then added, hilariously, "although I've never been to a game".

This was football being used as a political football: white Britons are intrinsically racist; men are the root of most evils; the working class are to be pitied, feared and kept in their place by tougher rules.

The incident rumbled on – it was headline news for a week, and online the lynch mob demanded lifelong bans from football and sackings, while some lost it altogether, baying for the Chelsea racists to be jailed for three years and fined the maximum £33,000 under French law.

Think about that: three years' chokey for cretinously shouting "we're racist, we're racist and that's the way we like it," and shoving a bloke off a train. A football fan I know whose attacker got a comparatively paltry six months after glassing him in the head might think that heavy-handed. But then his attack wasn't racially motivated – he's white and working-class – so maybe it wasn't as serious.

For those of us old enough to remember the bad old days of running football riots in town centres, when fans slashed each other with Stanley knives and carried snooker cues to matches as thinly-disguised weapons ("just been for a few frames with the lads, officer") the response to the Chelsea incident seemed baffling.

Yes, the game still has its problems – stamping out racism and homophobia are chief among them – but the hysterical claims that the sport is in some way returning to the 1980s, when right-wing hate groups recruited on the terraces is frankly laughable.

The Chelsea racist incident didn't just expose racism. It shone a light on something equally ugly, too: a class snobbery from a self-appointed intelligentsia who have a deep-rooted hatred of white, working-class men.

From the relentless mocking of "chavs", to the rage prompted by the country's work-shy, benefits-scrounging, obese underclass, from *Shameless* to *Benefits Street*, the working class are the bogeymen the snobs love to hate.

Dirty, racist, laddy, yobbish football is their sport of choice. Which is why the liberal elite spent the following days after the Chelsea story broke chanting themselves hoarse with their own shameful cry:

"We're classist, we're classist, and that's the way we like it!"

Martin Daubney is an award-wining editor, journalist, and broadcaster. He was the longest-serving editor of Loaded *magazine until fatherhood dragged him into the real world. He now educates teenagers on the potential dangers of online pornography and its role in sexual consent. You can follow him on Twitter @MartinDaubney*

FATHERS AND FATHERHOOD:

Who's the daddy?

Why I'm a Champion for Young Fathers

By Seany O'Kane

Time and time again when the subject of 'young fathers' is written about in the UK press, it's not surprising to see words used such as 'feckless', 'irresponsible' or 'absent' to describe them. Scandalous headlines often conjured up by reporters who have a total disregard for how complex the lives of young dads are, in some cases, a teenager embarking upon parenthood with no knowledge of what it means to be a man, never mind a dad.

If anything, the use of the word 'absent' when discussing young fathers should most-aptly be used when discussing just how little support exists for them.

As a specialist fatherhood practitioner, I dedicate my time to bettering the lives of young men who require support in relation to their parenting. Several years ago my organisation wanted to bridge a gap that existed within children and young people's services, particularly in South London. It's a gap that failed to address the needs of fathers in social care, specifically younger fathers from much more disenfranchised backgrounds.

Services to help these young men were much more limited than those in place to help young mothers, and what was hugely evident was when dads received support in the run-up to becoming a parent, they were more likely to be a prominent figure in their child's life. Therefore minimising the socio-economic risk factors often associated with children growing up without a father present.

The work I carry out ensures that young fathers are provided with a tailored service, helping to address their parenting needs. But even before I am able to get a young expectant dad to grasp his role in relation to fatherhood, it may be that he has other presenting factors that hinder his ability to appropriately safeguard his child.

For example, I have to assess each young or expectant father's level of need and work with them to achieve their parental goals, but when dealing with challenges such as gang involvement, homelessness, domestic abuse and drug misuse to name but a few, it certainly makes the role of a fatherhood practitioner much more intricate.

One of the biggest obstacles I encounter is not young men's reluctance to engage in the service – if anything it is their sheer determination to want to have a relationship with their child that contributes to achieving outcomes in a much quicker timescale – but the difficulties I face when working with external health and social care professionals to make changes to *their* practice.

Time and time again I witness young fathers whose children are part of a social care plan, yet they have not been asked to attend any child protection meetings arranged by social services to determine the outcome for their child. Young men in situations like this are left completely out of the picture, suggesting that the local authority must view young fathers to be part of the overall 'problem' within social care.

Yet I know that when a dad is considered in the future of his child's life, if he is part of a child protection plan and he himself is offered the right support to make changes for the better, his involvement can actually become a major part of the solution that helps decide the child's future.

The same can be said for young expectant fathers who are completely left out of antenatal care. I have assisted hundreds of young men who have expressed that they have never met their family midwife or ever received contact from her (in 2014 there were 103 practicing male midwives compared to 31,189 women).

Despite this unsettling information, the one other thing that all these young men had in common was that they 'did' want to be included, that they wanted to be acknowledged as the equal parent and that they just wanted to be validated in some way by the health professionals who were in place to ensure their unborn baby was properly cared for.

It's not uncommon for a midwife to carry out a home visit to a young couple's home and for the young man to feel that he isn't being included, that the midwife will focus all their attention towards mother and the unborn baby not even enquiring how he might be feeling or exploring what support he might benefit from.

It's common for young couples to undergo difficulties in their relationship following the birth of a baby, often resulting in separation. If the young man feels excluded as an equal parent right from the beginning and if he is being prevented from having contact with his child by the mother, the option to 'walk away' may appear to be in his best interests, when in reality and given the chance, he would like nothing more than to be there for his child. This applies to young dads I have assisted regardless of whether they are aged 14 or 25.

There needs to be a real cultural shift in the way health and social care throughout the UK considers the role of young fathers in the lives of their children and to ensure that the appropriate education is offered to students training to become midwives, social workers, health visitors etc. so that they have a genuine understanding of father-inclusive practice.

The end result will mean more confident health practitioners and more young fathers feeling included and equal in their child's lives, regardless of whether or not they are in a relationship with the child's mother. This will result in less children being separated from their fathers and contributing to overall healthy child development. Happier healthier children will mean a much happier healthier society for all of us. After all isn't that what we all want?

Seany O' Kane is a specialist fatherhood practitioner.

Dear Woman, Are You Happy Having More Parental Rights than Me?

By Glen Poole

Dear Woman,

Do you mind if I ask you something? I've often heard it said that you want men to do their fair share of parenting, but I don't think I've heard you say much about fathers' rights.

Sure, I've heard you say things like "it's not about parents' rights, it's about the child's rights" but that suggests that parents don't have any rights – and we do.

The rights we have as parents are defined not by our ability to parent, but by our sex. You say you want equality, so how do you feel about the fact that male parents have different and fewer rights than female parents?

I wonder if you're happy with this? I've not heard you raise it as a matter of concern. Maybe this is because you are unaware of the fact that I have fewer parental rights than you, because I'm a man.

If this is the case, then let me explain. If you and I met and had a one night stand that resulted in pregnancy this is how you'd have more rights than me (and let's be clear, I'm an experienced parent so there would be no concerns about my ability to be a great dad).

Firstly you have the right to decide if the child is born or not born – but as a man, I don't. I'm not suggesting we change that law, but upon this fact all other parental rights are built because "my body my rights" very quickly becomes "my baby my rights".

You'd also have the right to give birth to our child and give it up for adoption without consulting me. This means you have the right to choose if you want to walk away from your responsibility of parenting and paying for our child.

I don't.

If I chose to walk away , then you and the state could chase me for child maintenance for the next 18 years of our child's life, because while women have the right to walk away from being a parent when they think they've made a mistake, men don't have the same right to walk away from parenting. We are legally obliged to pay for our mistakes.

If you decided to keep our child you'd be granted automatic parental rights (even if you were the worst mum in the country); whereas I have no automatic parental rights (even if I'm the best dad in the country). That's right, the worst mum in the country has more automatic rights than the best dad.

Having parental rights means being able to make important decisions about our child's health, upbringing, religion and education – decisions I'd love to have an equal right to be involved in.

As the mother, you are the gatekeeper – your baby your rights remember? So you get to choose whether you are a full-time mum, a part-time mum or a full-time worker who gets help with childcare. It's your absolute right to make any of those choices and have the rest of us help pay for that choice, through our taxes, with various benefits, tax credits, maternity pay and childcare.

Do I have the same right? The right to choose whether I want to be a full-time dad to our child or a part-time dad or a full-time dad who gets help with childcare?

Do I have the right to make that choice as a man, the same choice you have the right to make as a woman?

No.

I have no automatic right to have any involvement in my child's life whatsoever. I have to negotiate with you, the mother – and/or the court – and take whatever role you/they are prepared to give me.

Even if we decided to take the plunge and raise our child together, you would still be the gatekeeper. Even with our recently improved shared parental leave rights, you still have more rights to paid parental leave than I do.

So if we did split up and end up in a custody battle, what would happen?

I've heard you say that the family courts aren't biased against men, that the courts simply favour the primary carer because this is in the child's best interest.

You are, of course right, that in a contested case the legal system would generally favour the person perceived to be the primary carer – but the reason more women are primary carers isn't simply because of cultural norms as I've heard you suggest.

Those norms are constantly changing and evolving,

but are still shaped by the fact that you, as a woman, have completely different parental rights to me and as such the vast majority of men don't stand a chance of being a primary or equal carer of their child and therefore stand little or no chance of ever winning a custody battle.

It seems that this status quo serves women's needs well, by which I mean your need to know that you can retain primary sovereignty over our children. Because "mother knows best". Because it's "your baby, your rights".

So though you say you want men and women to have equality, when I hear your deafening silence on the issue of fathers' rights, I'm left wondering – do you really want mums and dads to enjoy the privilege of sharing the rights and responsibilities of parenthood equally?

Because if this is the future we want to create for our sons and daughters together, then we're going to have to deal with the fact that mums and dads don't have equal rights.

With Kind Regards

A Man

Glen Poole is a leading expert on men's issues, UK co-ordinator for International Men's Day and author of the book Equality For Men. *He has established numerous grassroots projects for men and boys, is a regular media commentator and is news editor of* insideMAN *magazine.*

The Privilege and Sacrifice of Being a Stay-at-home Dad

By John Adams

I feel blessed to be a stay at home dad. It's a real honour to spend so much more time with my children compared to the majority of other men.

I won't pretend there aren't elements to my life I would change if given the opportunity. The school run springs to mind as something I could happily live without. I'd also welcome having more money and I'm desperately worried that my pension will be desperately underfunded.

Even though I have these worries, spending so much time with my kids is wonderful. If I think of last summer, we whiled away loads of time splashing about in a paddling pool. It's amazing how children, let alone adults, can have so much fun with something so simple.

I also have an old video stored on my phone of Helen playing in a park. The film is about three-and-a-half years old and was shot not long after I gave up full-time employment.

The film shows a magical moment. A train goes past on a nearby railway line and Helen, who was toddling down a path, stops in her tracks and says "Ooooooo, choo choo traayyynn!" The excitement in her voice is immeasurable.

In writing, that possibly doesn't appear too impressive. It was simply one of those lovely moments I'd never have been involved with if I'd been a full-time working dad.

There have been many other special moments; teaching the girls new words, encouraging Elizabeth to use a slide, baking cakes, going on 'number hunts' in the garden. Sure, my wife does many of these things too, but not nearly as much as I do.

I won't lie. It can be a very lonely existence. During office hours the only other person I generally get to see is my youngest daughter. As I alluded to above, it is also not a path to follow if you have a fondness for material possessions and wealth. You will be disappointed.

If, however, you want to do something that makes a statement and breaks rules, being a stay at home dad could be the route for you. You often hear mothers saying that childcare is very hard work and it's no different being a dad. My wife often tells me I have the more demanding role and she manages a huge number of people!

It's tough, financially hard and not always very sociable. Nonetheless it is rewarding and I wouldn't want things any other way.

John Adams is a married stay at home dad with two young children, one of the UK's leading Dad Bloggers and author of the book A modern father… and dad blogger. *As well as writing about equalities issues, family finances, men's style, days out and photography at Dad Blog UK, he also engages with Government and policymakers and regularly appears in the national media. You can visit his blog at www.dadbloguk. com and follow him on Twitter @dadbloguk*

Life Without Fatherhood

By Robin Hadley

In my research, I have been honoured to interview many men in the UK about their experiences of wanting to be a dad. All the meetings have been moving and reflected some aspect of my own thoughts and feelings regarding not becoming a father. Ironically, fatherhood is something that's simultaneously so easily achieved and important, that what it means not to become a father can't usually be talked about. So what do these men say?

Well, quite a lot and I can only give a flavour here of the depth and range that the impact of male involuntary childlessness has had on them.

Shane (33) blamed his two divorces on his desire for fatherhood. He saw the children as completing a family and himself as a person. *"You need to have the child to make you blossom as a person, as a family."*

Such was the impact of not achieving his dream of being a father by the age of 30 that, *"I was very, very depressed last year, suicidal."*

Many men wanted to repeat their own experience of being fathered, *"I saw him as a role model. For being a good Dad. Enjoying being a Dad. He was delighted to be a Dad. And I'd always assumed I'd become a Dad"* (Phil, 51).

Harry (64), a widower, had assumed he would die first and so when his partner of 39 years died two years ago he was left bereft, *"If we'd had children there would be a little piece of her still around"*. In addition, he now thought that because he was now a solo living, older man, he had to be careful *"I don't want someone to look saying, 'Watch that old man'."*

The fear of being seen a paedophile has been very strong with the men I've spoken to. Frank (56) single and solo living in a large rural village said:

"How is a man supposed to be a man?"

I believe his questions reflected the dramatic changes that have taken place socially and economically over the past 60 years. How are you supposed to be man in the 21st century? How are you supposed to be a young man, a middle-aged man, a young-old man, an old-old man? Is the breadwinner, provider, unemotional–yet–virile ideal man stereotype still valid? Was it ever? Where are the new resources that will provide the narratives to support men who 'don't quite fit'?

Finally, one of the most moving chats I had was with a man who had nothing to do with my research. 'John' (45) was laying a concrete ramp at my home. As we chatted I explained my research and about my own expectation to have been a Dad. John (45) stood up and looked me in the eye and said with real emotion in his voice, *"I don't know what I'd do without my kids."*

In that moment, we shared an understanding. Men talk – it is the listening and the hearing that is the difficult part.

Robin is a PhD researcher at Keele University studying the lives of men who wanted to be a dad but who aren't. He is a student member of the British Sociological Association, the British Society for Gerontology, and the Society of Reproductive and Infant Health.

How Can I Stop my Wife Chopping Off Our Son's Foreskin?

An Iranian father-to-be from London wrote to insideMAN *to ask for help stopping his wife circumcising their son. His letter to our readers is printed below. His article is anonymous to protect the identity of his son.*

Dear *insideMAN* Reader

Please can you help me?

I am an Iranian man living in London just days away from becoming a father for the first time. I feel so special about his birth. I feel he is going to be a very precious gift to me. I can't wait to see him and hold him tight in my arms. As a proud father I would like, to the best of my ability, to protect and nurture him and that includes protecting him from being circumcised.

Unfortunately, my wife disagrees with me and insists that she will have him circumcised just like her son (my step son) from her first marriage. I feel powerless and cannot sleep at night because of this issue. My wife will not listen to the reasons why I want to protect him from circumcision. I have tried to approach her from different angles but I keep hitting a brick wall.

So what can I do?

I come from a diverse family, my mum is an open-minded Muslim, my dad is an anti-religion atheist whose parents came to the UK from Iran in the 1970s, just before the Islamic revolution. I started living in the UK permanently myself 14 years ago and while people think of me as Muslim, because I was born in Iran, I am not. I am an atheist and only believe in balance and justice in the universe.

As parents I believe we should not stamp our religion, culture, tradition or opinions on our children without their consent. I find circumcision totally barbaric. I strongly believe circumcision trauma leaves a deep blueprint on the subconscious mind and soul of a baby. I believe that human beings are born in a complete form of perfection. If there is a nose to breathe through or a pair of eyes to see, there is certainly a reason for the foreskin to be there. A boy's penis is the very centre of his manhood, why would anyone want to mess with it and reduce it? I feel very strongly that we should ban circumcision, especially in Europe.

Sadly, for some strange reason, most Iranian women support male circumcision. A good friend of mine who is a highly educated lawyer, born to an Iranian family and raised in the UK, recently gave birth to a lovely little boy. I could not believe her strong views about circumcision. Her main concern was the beauty and the similarity of his penis to her husband! It seems Iranian women take the same approach to circumcision as they have to plastic surgery. They think it's a nose job!

My mother also supports circumcision, even though she is a very open-minded, flexible, modern woman for her generation. She heard me trying to explain to my wife why I want to prevent our son from being circumcised and she told me afterwards that I should "give in gracefully and let her do it"!

My mum's thinking is that my wife is going to do it anyway and there is a positive side to circumcision which, according to my mum is this – my baby's willy will look the same as mine and my stepson's and prevent any confusion he might feel in future if he compares his penis to ours!

I said to her, "Mum, how often do you see me and my brothers and Dad sitting at a dinner table, comparing our bits with each other?" We are, of course, all circumcised. I have never questioned my parents about this because they did what they thought was right at the time. I don't have strong feelings about being circumcised myself, as long as I can remember I have always been this way, but I have always wondered how it would feel if I wasn't circumcised and I never heard of an uncircumcised man who wants to have it done.

But now I have the knowledge, I am conscious and I know the fact my father is against it too. I feel I must do everything I can to protect my son. I won't have any issues if he decides to do it when he is older but that is his decision to make, it's his body and it's his choice.

But my wife's mind is made up. She is a Christian woman of Iranian background, so her reasons are not religious, I would say it's more cultural and mainly cosmetic. She plans to have him circumcised in a private clinic in Harley Street. I cannot begin to describe how distressed I am about the whole thing. It's almost taking away the excitement of having a baby and becoming a dad.

I am in desperate need of help and support. I've been in touch with the charity NORM UK and *insideMAN* magazine and I'm going to try the NHS too. I'd welcome support from any organisations or charities who understand my point of view and I'd like to know my legal rights as a father. I'd also like to hear from other parents who have been in a similar situation.

Please help me, I want to protect my son from circumcision before it's too late.

Footnote:

The author was contacted by *insideMAN* ahead of his article's inclusion in this book for an update on the family's circumstances. His response is below:

The support I received through *insideMAN* was invaluable, they were the only people who seemed to understand what I was going through. Sadly, after taking legal advice, I felt the only way to keep my family together was to go along with my wife's wishes.

At least I could be there to support my son, rather than taking the risk that she would do it behind my back. So we went to a doctor in Harley Street together and I cried throughout the procedure and he was crying his eyes out too. The moment the operation was over I snatch him from the nurse's arms and whispered in his ear that he will never have to go through such trauma ever again.

I couldn't believe how much blood was in his nappy and I had to take him to a second specialist to find out if he was okay, because the first doctor didn't tell us what to expect.

I still feel frustrated and heartbroken that I was unable to protect my son, and since the operation I have recently developed alopecia, which I think was caused by the stress of this situation.

I'm sad to say that the sparkle from my relationship with my wife has completely gone and I have been so deeply touched by what happened that I don't think it can be repaired.

But my son is such a delight. I'm being a really hands-on dad and we've bonded really well. He loves being in my company and when I return from work he cries out as soon as he hears my voice.

He is the best thing to ever happen to me. We have bonded so well, it feels like he knows how much I care about him and when he is old enough and will share this article with him so he knows what happened.

Grandfather, Father, Brother, Remembrance

By Dr. Max Mackay-James

This is a story that lives in a photograph. It is an old picture in a dusty frame, and I think of it sitting on chests of drawers for many years with nobody bothering to look at it much. But now I do.

The picture is of my father when he was fourteen. We all called him 'Bob' rather than Dad. I don't know why, and I've never found out where the name came from. He wasn't a Robert or anything – his real name was Peter. Growing up, I didn't know anyone else whose Dad was called Bob. The name was a bit magical, it made him special in my eyes.

It is a studio photograph and the picture is set up as a profile silhouette with the photographer lighting Bob's face from the side against a black background. You can see the photographer's name at the bottom on the right – Noelfreda (with the accent on the 'e'). And you can also just see the date on the left – 1930 (which is how I know he was fourteen years old when the photograph was taken).

He is wearing a white peaked hat, and there are markings on his epaulette signifying that he is a Royal Navy cadet. I imagine the formal photograph was taken to mark his completion of the first part of his education and training to become a naval officer. Perhaps he is wearing the uniform for the first time.

So it captures an important transition moment in my father's life, and his rite of passage from boyhood education to young adult life. It is one of the many things I love about this photograph. I don't know if the photographer asked Bob to tilt his head forward for the photograph or he chose to do this himself. Whatever I also love is his humility in this gesture of looking down.

The young man has passed through the cave of darkness and is emerging into the light.

I get a timeless quality, the sun is forever rising in front of my father, even if he does not wish at this moment to raise his head to look directly at it. It always gives me a feeling of confidence: here is my father as my humble guide across the years. Even now I am old, indeed old enough to be Bob's grandfather in this photograph, I still get this reassurance from him, from the youth entering adult life in humility with head bowed, and forever showing me the way.

Except by not looking at the light directly himself and looking down, and there is a second possibility. Perhaps he is not refusing to look towards the future. Maybe he is in a place of darkness and is refusing to look at the past from where the light comes from the wreckage of history which is on fire. After all Bob was born in 1916. He is a child of the First World War.

In this second possibility the flames of the past are burning in the darkness of the night. The future is being denied my father and his head is turned away from what is to come. Maybe this turning away is actually an act of wisdom on his part. In 1939 he was 23, and by then a Royal Navy officer on active service on destroyer warships. So he was pitched straight into the Second World War, and the ships he was on got involved in fighting, first in the Mediterranean and then on Russian convoys which accompanied merchant ships to Murmansk in 1942.

I don't know what he saw of the horrors of war, and like many men of his generation, and the one before, he refused to talk about it. I also never saw him wear his string of medals. Like in the photograph his head remained bowed and he kept silent. And each year in November around Remembrance Day, I find myself conflicted in my feelings about his submissive gesture in the photograph.

Yes, on the one hand in his submission I do feel a personal sense of pride for what he did, and the service and sacrifice of his generation which, I have no doubt, has given me a better life. And on the other hand, I hate his gesture of submission to war and the violent and destructive aspects of men, and the masculine systems of authority whose acts of aggression and folly lead to the death of so many, and wrecked and traumatised the lives of so many others.

Above all I hate his silence, because of course when you don't speak about shadow things – including the horrors of war – you can't speak of other loving things as much as you want to either.

And still it goes on today. As I get older, and especially during the Remembrance Day month, I want to speak out more and more passionately against these old aggressive and violent patterns of men and masculinity. I need this photograph of Bob to remind and show me how to be different. Inside we men are vulnerable – of course we are! Inside, my father says, men want none of these legacies of violence and long to be free of them.

I use the photograph of Bob this way to cut through my sometimes conflicted feelings about the past, and what always shines through to me is the tenderness on my father's young face. So I speak out because I know there is a better legacy from history for men than war. It is this tenderness.

And so I also know Bob's gift of love.

Max is a retired GP living in West Dorset. He is a graduate of London University's Department of Palliative Care and is passionate about growing a grassroots-up 'quiet revolution' for better ageing and dying, caring and loss. He is director of the Conscious Ageing charity – a small charity that is 100% community owned and run, which carries out targeted work in Dorset and London. Conscious Ageing charity is home of D&ealog – which aims to build communities of better experience, good practice and compassion for ageing, dying, caring and loss.

HEALTH AND WELLBEING:

What's going on inside men?

Men, You Can Recover from the Edge of Suicide

By James Withey

I'm sat on a chair in my room on a psychiatric ward; the sun is reaching through the branches of the tree behind me and daubing a beautiful light show on the wall. A year ago I was a Training Officer with a large charity delivering courses including the life-saving ASIST (Applied Suicide Intervention Skills Training) to groups of social care workers and now I'm on 15-minute suicide watch.

Depression crept up behind me and broke me in 2011 after a series of events that made my soul collapse. I was fortunate in some ways. I had worked in counselling and social care all my life and knew that I was unwell; I also knew that I was entitled to support.

I had taught others about suicide; how men are more likely to die by suicide, how men want help but find it hard to find the services to match and that suicidal thoughts are temporary but feel permanent.

When I was first ill I spent four nights in the Maytree Sanctuary for the Suicidal in London, which saved my life and gave me time to reflect on the notion of recovery. Until my time in Maytree only one mental health professional had told me I could recover from depression;

this was a student nurse who was accompanying the full-time workers and leaving the flat she turned, smiled and said, 'James, you can recover from this.' At Maytree I had a chance to think about this and the importance of hope.

Depression tried to steal everything from me and temporarily succeeded. It took my career, my memory, my concentration, my confidence, my sense of humour, friendships, sleep, eating, motivation and one of my biggest losses was reading. I used to be an avid reader, a few novels a month and suddenly nothing, I couldn't read a page, I couldn't read half a page. I borrowed some books from the library but couldn't get past the first sentence and the more I tried the more of a failure I felt.

What I wanted was to read small pieces of writing that would give me some hope that I could get through; I wanted to hear about other people's experiences of emerging through the treacle–like existence that is depression. This is how the idea of Recovery Letters came about because I wondered, if this would have helped me, would it would help others too?

Recovery Letters is a simple premise; people recovering from depression write a letter to those that are currently suffering. I wrote the initial letter and then used twitter to ask other people to write subsequent letters. The response has been incredible, including men who have explained that starved of sleep, late at night, the letters have helped them survive until the morning.

As a man I know the difficulties of opening up; after

one disastrous phone call to a helpline at 3 a.m. where the helpline worker didn't say anything to me, I vowed never to call again and that night took an overdose of sleeping pills. I'm not blaming that helpline worker who no doubt was anxious and unsure of what to say, it was maybe their first call and they just wanted to help. My point is that men need to be engaged in different ways, we need to understand how hard it is for men to open up. Our duty is to provide a variety of methods of support so that the right fit can be found.

Talking about suicide is also hard. When Stephen Fry was asked recently why he didn't tell close friends about his feelings before a recent suicide attempt, he responded by explaining that it's like admitting the most embarrassing and mortifying thing you could reveal, so big is the shame.

He said: "*Think of your very best friend. Very, very best friend. Suppose you suddenly noticed you had a massive and really disturbing genital wart... would you show it to your very best friend*?"

The Recovery Letters website has been running since September 2012 and we now have dozens of letters on the site from people who have taken the time and effort to sit down and write to people they've never met. They benefit too, writing down thoughts, feelings and reaching out to others helps to cement one's own recovery. No-one is paid any money to write or read the letters, yet everyone benefits.

I use the letters myself. My recovery is up and down, as most people's is, and because depression blinds you to the truth, I will often sit down and remind myself that if the people who wrote these letters are alive, living their lives alongside or after depression then I can do the same, and I do.

James Withey founded the mental health website Recovery Letters after facing depression. You can read the letters at www.therecoveryletters.com and follow on Twitter @ RecoveryLetters.

The Taboo of Eating Disorders in Men, One Man's Story

By Craig Edwards

How do you explain to someone that you don't feel right? How do you explain a mental health problem to someone when you are unsure if you really have one yourself?

This was how I was feeling during my adolescent years. I always felt as though there was a missing piece of jigsaw inside me. I was a child whose own Father had walked out, never to be seen again. Was this a trigger? But that was when I was three and here I was at twelve feeling that the only way I could begin to put that jigsaw together was through an eating disorder.

Was the fact that I was now self-harming, in a way making up for what I believed was just me not feeling right for years mentally? These were important years and I didn't have my biological father there to guide me, was this finally taking its toll on me? I needed and wanted to escape the feeling of being rejected as a baby, but I didn't understand the full concept of that until I was much older, my way of doing so was to become a young man coping and learning how to deal with bulimia.

To the outside world I was a happy child, but if you were to look back now you would say that I was also very needy. I liked to be liked, we all do, but rejection was hard for me to handle. If I felt rejected then my bulimia would increase, if I felt worthless then the intrusive thoughts in later years would increase and then stabilise, to the point of me wanting to get my own back on my pain by secretly continuing with my bulimia. My body and mind felt trapped in a vicious circle of destruction.

When I was a young man and experiencing an eating disorder, I learned to stay in control of when, where and how often I would fall into my dark moments. But keeping my eating disorder secret had an adverse effect on my mental state, so something had to give and for me that led to me becoming more depressed and having intrusive thoughts about ending my life.

One day those thoughts all became too much and after spending time in a mental health hospital, I decided that I had to change. I had to remember what I had around me and not what was taken away from me, and that I had the love of my family.

My other love was music and for me listening to music in hospital made me learn to really listen to it. In a place with complete chaos at times I would take myself off to my room, play music and forget the world. I'd remind myself that the one person who could really help me become well again was me. Instead of wanting love from a person who clearly didn't want to give it to me, I learned to channel the love I wanted myself.

Things for me are now different, I turn all my past lived experience into being a mental health nurse and, understanding what it is like to become suffocated in your own deep thoughts, I help others who are going through something similar.

Eating disorders in men, just like depression, should not be a taboo subject. I hope that by raising awareness, others will be encouraged to seek professional help too. After all, if we really care for our friends and family then we should learn to read between the lines and see when they need help too.

It's not that easy I know but when you're experiencing a mental health problem you want those people to understand what you are going through before you can begin to find that road to recovery. It is a hard one, but acceptance of mental health really can be that simple.

Typically eating disorders are perceived to be conditions that affect only women, however between 10 and 25 per cent of people who experience eating disorders are male. For more information on the issue visit 'Men Get Eating Disorders Too', a charity that seeks to raise awareness of eating disorders in men and to support sufferers, carers and their families.

Life as a Disabled Man, what is Normal Anyway?

By Dr Jon Hastie

I don't consider myself a typical man, by any definition. Sure, there are certain things I can tick off that increase my sense of manhood – I live in my own flat, I have a job, my own car, friends who I see regularly, and even a pet I take care of. My interests include gaming, IT, film, theatre and politics. This is how I see myself, and to me this feels fairly normal. But I also see the reactions of other "normal" people whenever they see me, and that reminds me each time that my life is remarkable in some way. Reactions vary from the sublime to the ridiculous. You have the random passers-by at the theatre who congratulate me for getting out (this has happened twice in the last year). Or the people that very respectfully go out of their way to ignore the obvious visual differences they are presented with and pretend they don't notice. All very polite, but you know that their internal dialogue is having a Fawlty-esque "Don't Mention the War" moment.

Clearly I'm different then, even though my life feels pretty normal to me. Of course, when you get right down to it, the details sound very different from your average person. I have Duchenne Muscular Dystrophy, a genetic muscle wasting condition which began in early childhood and causes my muscles to waste away. It's something I have always known, which made me physically slower and weaker than my non-disabled peers from age three or four, and has got slowly and steadily worse over time. Walking got harder and harder until I started using a wheelchair at age 10. My arms and legs continued to get weaker until I could no longer lift heavy objects, then couldn't open doors, then raise my hand to scratch my face or brush my hair. Now, I can only just use a computer and drive my wheelchair. Breathing got harder in my early 20s, as I started having to use a ventilator overnight, then during the afternoons, and, in the last year, 24 hours a day. I take medication to keep my heart ticking over.

I'm not sure there is such a thing as a typical man these days, but obviously it isn't me. I would hope we've moved beyond the rather simplistic traditional stereotype of a man as very physical, dominant, gruff and emotionally simple, but even the alternative types of man that have emerged in recent narratives don't really represent me. The stereotype I suppose I most identify with is the geek, an identity made increasingly mainstream by shows such as *The Big Bang Theory*, where intelligence is prized more than physicality. Even then, the geek identity misses the areas of my life shaped by disability and is very far from my reality.

Whether modern geek or traditional man, there are common traits we associate with manliness, which have been less than straightforward to realise in my own life. Independence and autonomy are key. Modern men are often mocked for living with their parents beyond a certain age, for not having a way to support themselves to become autonomous. It still feels like society sees a reliance on professionals (nurses, care assistants, etc.) for help with personal care as emasculating. Men are still defined by what they do in employment, and power still seems to have a degree of manliness attached to it. There's still a perception that men are more like men if they are confident and forthright, i.e. they have "balls". All of these aspects are much harder as someone living with Duchenne.

I have strived to achieve these qualities, as I've jumped through bureaucratic hoops and challenged unfavourable decisions to get a care package that allows me to live independently, to get out and about and go to work. I've accepted financial support from family to get an accessible home, car and wheelchair that meets my needs. I have learnt how to be a good employer of personal care assistants. I've learnt how to manage a complex health condition by myself. I've taken up volunteering when initially unable to find work, to build up connections and prove my ability, to eventually secure a paid job I'm proud of. A far more complex route to achieving autonomy and independence than your average non-disabled man, and all just to feel "normal". I would in fact contend that overcoming these challenges makes me something more than just average!

There are some things you simply have to accept. I cannot be physically expressive, passionate, good with my hands or physically strong. I need personal care assistants to perform basic personal care tasks. I need to be fed, washed, and helped to use the toilet by care staff. While I am quite used to this by now, initially it was hard to surrender to the reality and accept that it didn't make me less of a man. Non-disabled men I speak to are equally fascinated and appalled by the very idea of having someone wipe your bum for you. I'm not sure why wiping your bum is so specifically important, but it's the first thought everyone seems to have!

To cope with my dependence, I often seek to establish my manliness in different ways. Vital to this is the need to have choice and control over the care I receive. To do this, I have a personal budget from the NHS (previously social services) to buy in my own support. This means I am the boss. I might need someone to wipe my bum for me, but I choose who is worthy enough for this job, I pay them for it, and by doing so am financially supporting them to live their lives too. Sadly, many with Duchenne do not get to choose their care providers, and as our recent research has shown, are often treated like children by a social care profession ill-equipped to look after young men appropriately. I've had to work hard to prevent that from happening, and it's not something everyone knows how to do.

I know that I cannot demonstrate manliness by offering a physical, passionate love affair to a potential partner, or physical strength. But as an individual, I can use my intelligence to exercise power, and to achieve the outcomes I want. I can show strength in other ways, in emotional stability, maturity and self-awareness. By learning from the barriers I have experienced and the ways in which I have overcome them, I have developed a greater empathy for others experiencing their own issues. I can have in-depth, thoughtful discussions and feel more in touch with my feelings, having had no choice but to face up to the uncomfortable reality of physical decline. This feels pretty manly to me as it requires great inner strength.

I couldn't have done this alone, and I hugely value and appreciate the support I have received along the way. Some people might see this as less masculine than doing it all alone. That has never been an option, and I think it's an unhelpful aim to aspire to. Pride is something that should be challenged, not welcomed. Is it manly to try and chop down a tree with your bare hands? Or just stupid? Far better to accept your own limitations and use the full range of tools available to you. Family support, care assistants, wheelchairs, ventilators, cough-assist machines – these are the tools that were available to me and if I hadn't used them, I'd certainly be dead by now.

It's not all been a positive experience. As a disabled man, there are many barriers thrown up by society that have restricted my potential, and I haven't been able to overcome or compensate for. I have missed so many social opportunities as venues or even friends' houses are completely inaccessible to me. My career development has been restricted to local opportunities by the barriers of working, living and travelling around London. Social attitudes towards dating disabled people has meant I've spent most of my life single. I haven't been able to be as much of a man as I wanted to be.

In terms of realising my identity, the fact that I'm gay adds a further complication. There's no road map for what being a gay disabled man could look like. I've been so concerned about being seen as less of a man by the care assistants and family that are ever-present that I didn't come out until I was 31. It was a shock as no-one expects a disabled person to be gay too. Again due to poor venue accessibility, I haven't been able to participate in the gay scene since then and have only a handful of gay friends.

I don't think being masculine should be defined as having a job, strength or power. I think we should as a society strive for a much more inclusive, positive definition. It should be about making choices, and about having inner strength to adapt, evolve and learn about ourselves as men. To use all the tools available to us to live our lives well, not just for ourselves but the benefit of all parts of society, particularly the most vulnerable.

I accept that I'm not a typical man. Although my life is normal to me, I recognise it's very different from everyone else. I used to insist that my disability didn't define me. But the more severe my condition becomes, the more I realise that this simply isn't true. Of course, key personality traits would remain the same, whether I was disabled or not, and many of the interests I have I would still have as a non-disabled person. But the notion that overcoming the barriers I have faced, and the ongoing experience of being partially excluded from society has not shaped my identity in significant ways is simply nonsense. Disability has allowed me to become strong and powerful in non-traditional ways that are not easily available to the average, conventional man. If other men could begin to comprehend what can be gained by meeting adversity head on and the value it brings I think there would be a lot less misery in the world.

Jon has Duchenne Muscular Dystrophy, a muscle-wasting condition that primarily affects men and boys. He is policy and communications lead at independent lives and trustee of DMD pathfinders.

What are Men Really Looking for when They Watch Internet Porn?

By Patrick McCurry

"The soul often manifests itself in the sexual areas of life." – Thomas Moore

Internet porn is an increasing issue among the male, heterosexual clients I see, and one that can cause a lot of shame as well as impacting on intimate relationships.

Some couples and individuals may have a comfortable relationship with porn and it may be something they enjoy making a part of their sex lives. But for many men it can become something secretive and taboo, which they turn to not simply because of the pleasure it offers but also as a way of escaping difficult feelings.

The easy and free accessibility of internet porn (and the range of sexual activity one can view) means that it can quickly become an instant hit for men who are not feeling good about themselves.

When the need for that 'hit', for that escape, becomes a regular way of handling difficult feelings internet porn use can become a problem both for the individual and his partner if he is in a relationship.

For me the interesting part is not just what a man

may be escaping by using internet porn, but what he may, unconsciously, be seeking.

To explore this one must ask the individual what he is drawn to in the experience, how he actually feels in the midst of it. Male clients tell me they feel excitement and passion when they are lost in internet porn, that they enjoy the secretive and rule-breaking atmosphere.

Some also feel they are giving themselves a treat or reward and even that they feel somehow nurtured by or attended to by the women they watch engaging in sex.

For some men there is also a pleasure in seeing women treated in a dominating, or even humiliating, way sexually and this may be tapping into unresolved angry feelings towards women that go back to childhood.

Part of the work with these clients is about exploring with them what the porn gives them and whether that is a sign that there is something missing from the rest of their lives and relationships. If they feel excitement and passion using porn, is there a boredom or flatness in the rest of their life or relationships? If so, how can they bring some excitement into other areas of their life?

I would be interested in what might be holding the man back from bringing these energies into his life. Did he grow up with the message that it was somehow not OK for him to express excitement or passion, for example?

If the man feels somehow looked after or attended to by the women in porn videos, does this mean he feels that is lacking in his other relationships with women? Can he ask for these needs to be met in other relationships and can he begin to look after or attend to himself in healthier ways?

For the man who is aroused by women being dominated or treated in a humiliating way I would be interested in how he felt his childhood excitement, anger and sexuality were treated by women. Did he feel those parts were not acceptable and did he feel humiliated by his mother or other females when he showed those energies and emotions?

What I'm aware of when I hear the stories of men who have problematic relationships with porn is how the activity, as well as an escape is also a movement towards something. This 'something' is often about feeling alive, connected to one's excitement, feeling connected to and accepted by a woman.

Even the man who is drawn to porn that demeans women is, in a distorted way, trying to establish a connection with the feminine. If those feelings of anger and powerlessness, with regard to women, can be made more conscious they can then be worked with.

As psychotherapist and author Thomas Moore says, in his book *The Soul of Sex*, many of the people who came to see him had sexual concerns, "which eventually were revealed as containers of the central mysteries of the person's life".

Patrick McCurry is a psychotherapist with practices in Eastbourne and east London. He sees individuals and couples and has been trained in integrative psychosynthesis.

Male Genital Mutilation, One Man's Story

By Patrick Smyth

I and my sister were born in the late 50's in the UK. Soon after I was born my parents taught me what it is to be discriminated against.

They saw to it that my foreskin was cut off and tossed away, but nothing was cut off my sister's body when she was subsequently born. If I had been born a female I would still have all the genitals I was born with, just as my sister still has.

We hear a lot about FGM and rightly so, as it is an abomination. Sadly, many think that male circumcision is performed for religious and medical reasons: so it can't be harmful. The truth is that all those men and boys who were circumcised without their personal consent are the victims of the theft of a functional and erogenous body part.

You do not enrich the life of a man by cutting a part of his body off, you make that man a poorer man, even though he may not realise it because he has never known any different.

I recently spotted the following comment in response to an online petition against infant male circumcision: "I was circumcised as an adult... I can confirm that it royally fucks up a man's sexuality."

This came as no surprise to me since it was as obvious as my lack of a foreskin that my wife was enjoying a more 'earth-moving' sexual experience than me. We are now separated after spending almost 30 years together and I reflect that sexual issues were very much the undoing of our marriage. My sex life was not what it should have been. I now live alone and am a chastened man.

It is my personal belief that all infants, whether they be male or female, should enjoy the basic right to be born unto parents that do not feel it is their right to modify the genitalia of their offspring.

My late parents felt that it was their right to condone my circumcision as an infant without medical necessity. This is something that has caused me considerable pain and anguish and I shall eternally regret. It should have been my own decision as to whether or not I chose to give up an intimate and personal part of my body, because once it is done, it is done.

Children are in the custody of their parents until they reach maturity and are not their property. I am not Jewish or Muslim, but there are men I know of that were born unto Jewish/Muslim parents that also resent the fact that they suffered the same indignity of forced circumcision.

The majority of men in this world are genitally intact and perfectly content with their status. I believe that it is a profound injustice that there is not statutory legal protection for all infant boys against non-therapeutic circumcision (such as there is for girls in the UK, US and elsewhere), regardless of the religious affiliation of their parents.

If men want to be circumcised for religious reasons let them volunteer for it once they are adults, and can give meaningful consent.

Patrick Smyth is trustee and secretary of NORM UK, an organisation that works to advance the education of the public in all matters relating to circumcision and other forms of surgical alteration of the genitals, including alternative treatments and the provision of information and advice.

The Journey Towards being a Lonely Old Man Starts Young

By Jim Pollard

A recent report from Independent Age suggests that increasing numbers of men are facing loneliness and isolation in old age and that with more and more older men living alone – a predicted rise of 65% to 1.5 million by 2030 – the number of men with such feelings looks set to increase rapidly.

The media coverage featured often touching interviews with older men. Although I'm still many years from retirement, and it is hard to admit, their stories struck a chord with me. It also feels very ungracious. (And I'm certainly not blaming anyone but myself.) I am in the luckiest fraction of this planet's population – a roof over my head, not poor and I know I'm loved by both my family and my long-term partner who accepts me as I am – so what am I whining about? But I say this not to whine but because I wonder if others feel the same. The report talks of older men but, for some of us anyway, the road to loneliness begins earlier.

The report says that isolation is being by yourself. Loneliness is not liking it. We all want to be alone sometimes. Indeed, being happy in your own company is often considered a good thing. Especially in men.

But too much, even of a good thing, can be dangerous. Addictive. We don't admit to being lonely, we just tell ourselves we're loners. (Perhaps it's no coincidence that my job – writing – necessitates vast periods of time on your own.)

It should be easy to tackle loneliness. Just phone someone. So why can't I? (The rational part of your mind tells you that your friend will be as pleased to hear from you as you would from him.) Why, since I write, can't I even think of something to post on Facebook? When I was single I had many lonely Saturday nights, never phoning friends because I assumed they had something better to do. Now, thanks to social media, I know they have something better to do. Or, at least, that's the impression – and it makes it harder to make that leap of faith and get in touch.

Most of my friends date back years to school and university. In other words, they date back to a time when I had an ascribed place in the world. Over time, things can change – values, incomes, locations, lifestyles – or the little differences – in intelligence, talent, ambition – can become bigger. You can, even with the best intentions, drift apart.

As an adult you have to find your place in the world yourself and if you struggle in that, you can become detached. When you become detached you start seeing the differences rather than the similarities between yourself and others: you're not exactly a journalist, you're not really an author. You find excuses for disengagement. I lived abroad for a long time. If I didn't fit in there, well, it was the language. That story won't wash back home.

'I am condemned to be free', said Jean Paul Sartre, a very unhappy man, but we know exactly what he meant. Only you can give your life a meaning. We do it most often through family, work, a hobby, interest or pastime: the bloke who will do anything for his kids, the driven careerist, the guy who hates his job but loves running. It is giving meaning to our lives in these ways that gives us a place in the world. But this alone isn't enough. It's not an end in itself. What me and perhaps a lot of other men have forgotten (if we ever knew), is that through the things we make meaningful we also develop and nurture the only thing that really makes us happy – relationships.

Never mind Sartre, look no further than the film *Up In The Air* when George Clooney's self-obsessed character says: 'If you think about it, your favourite memories, the most important moments in your life… were you alone?'

The answer, as George realises, is no. It's not the time alone that makes you lonely. It's the neglect of relationships that too much time alone results in. Don't realise it and you could be on a lonely road: lone wolf at 30, isolated at 40, lonely at 50. Do realise it and that's when you need to start building bridges. (And hope you haven't burned too many.) But that's another article.

Jim Pollard is a writer and editor with an interest in men's health. He edits menshealthforum.org.uk

WAR AND VIOLENCE:

Take it like a man

Why Kitchener's Finger Gives Me the Arsehole

By Dan Bell

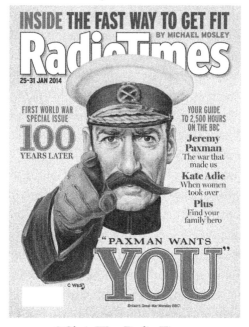

©Chris West/Radio Times.

If there is one image from the First World War that's more iconic than any other, it is the Big-Brother stare and jabbing index finger of Lord Kitchener.

A century after the propaganda campaign ended, it's an image that is still all around us – the original now re-versioned and re-deployed on everything from coffee mugs and duvet covers, to jaunty student union flyers, tourist T-shirts and even to satirise David Cameron's Big Society.

It's so ubiquitous, in fact, as to have morphed into kitsch; the lazy go-to stock image for anyone who wants to knock-up a quick call to action.

But that accusatory forefinger isn't just an old bit of Keep-Calm-And-Carry-On retro irony. It stands for a unique and brutal form of discrimination. What's more, no-one either seems to notice or even care if they do.

The explicit purpose of the Kitchener recruitment poster was to shame every man of enlistment age who saw it into signing up. It was a demand by the state that men and boys risk death and trauma or face becoming a social pariah if they refused.

In short, it is an expression of ultimate, state-sanctioned, socially-reinforced gendered discrimination – total control of the state over the bodies of one half of the population.

I'd like to suggest that you put yourself in the position of a young man walking past those posters back in 1914.

As he walked down the high street, or waited for a bus, or went into a post office or a library, that finger was pointing at him.

But more than that, no matter how crowded those streets and buildings were with women, each of them remained entirely untouched by its accusation. Every man, however, would have felt that finger jabbing into his chest, those eyes boring into the back of his head.

And that young man would have felt the force of that

shame from the women who stood beside him too.

Kitchener's two-dimensional jab in the chest was made flesh by women's unique power to shame men for cowardice, a power that was ruthlessly exploited by the state and often enthusiastically adopted by women themselves.

Take a moment to think about it. An image that makes no explicit gendered statement at all – the simple words "Your Country Needs You" makes no reference to men or women – yet it was nonetheless totally understood only to apply to men.

That silent image was a manifestation of society's deep and iron-clad demands on men and the stigma that stalked them should they refuse to conform.

The shame of male cowardice must have felt like the weight of the atmosphere, so close to your skin that you couldn't feel where your body stopped and it began.

The fact that now – fully 100 years later – we glibly fail to notice that this is the core meaning of that poster says a lot about how we view male suffering and disadvantage today.

Take a look at the *Radio Times'* interpretation of the Kitchener poster on its front page. Then notice the headline for Kate Adie's two-page spread on women entering the work force as a result of WW1.

Which one of these is most sensitive to the gendered sacrifices of the First World War?

If we can't, even today, see conscription and pervasive social stigma as a gendered injustice against men, what else must we be blind to?

Are the Dead Really Being Heard on Remembrance Sunday?

By Mike Payne

With the anniversary of the Great War, and the wars in Iraq and Afghanistan, remembrance seems to be more valued in society than when I served. I also sense something missing despite many thoughtful and respectful acts. I sense the voices of the dead are not being fully heard.

This year in particular there have been images of poppies in railways stations and public places, most notably the field of poppies around the Tower of London which was beautiful, powerful and reflective. However it concerns me that many of these displays feel like the hand of marketing, not the soul of the War Poet.

With the poppy season extended into October you now have a situation where those in the public eye wear poppies, indeed have to wear them, yet at the same time they are noticeable by their absence on the high street. I would expect more not less poppies being worn given there is more support.

Maybe there is a disconnect between what is felt and how the poppy is perceived, maybe the season is too long. Maybe it is because of the emotional and mental juggling act of not supporting recent wars, alongside a genuine desire to support those fighting them. Is there a sense we look to the past yet are not addressing the repeat patterns today?

It is difficult for serving soldiers to speak out, not least because they are willingly subservient to the democratic authority and are censored.

Had I been killed on operational tour it would have been while trying, imperfectly, to create a safe framework where people could make daily choices safely – for example, pop down to M&S or vote without being kneecapped. To me that self-evidently includes freedom of choice in whether or not to wear a poppy, or indeed a white or a black one.

For me wearing the red poppy includes the reality that war is primal and revolting and not glorious. For me remembrance is best served by wearing the poppy for a short period for collective impact, not a damp whimper over a few weeks.

In the British Armed Forces there are 10 principles of war, the first being: *Selection and Maintenance of the Aim*. Apply that to Iraq and Afghanistan: in Iraq there were no 'Weapons of Mass Destruction' and politicians routinely say they were deceived into voting for war because the prime minster misled Parliament. Yet the political class have not resolved this and all wear their poppy. How would the dead feel about that?

What if alongside the Tower of London display was the rotting corpse of a soldier, the smell hitting the back of your throat as you look on. The reality of a dead young man – a son, brother, father, lover, friend. Where is the essence of that element of remembrance being held? The *never again*, or if you must, *do it properly next time*.

Is it time to take the marketing out of remembrance so that the voices of the dead can be fully heard?

Mike Payne is an ex-serviceman who now works to support people living with the hidden impact of armed conflict or military service. For more information visit the unload website at www.unload.org.uk

Breaking the Silence over Male Victims of Domestic Violence

By Chris Good

Within minutes I found myself passing the university bars. Music pounded through the night air alongside the sound of enthusiastic chatter from punters. Dodging a taxi, I crossed the road and continued toward the shop. My nose throbbed and blood still trickled down over my chin onto my, already, stained T-shirt. It wasn't stopping.

Head down, I attempted to pass a group walking toward me but suddenly felt hands on my shoulders.

"Oh my god, mate, are you okay?"

I told them I was fine but the guy was a paramedic and stood me to the side. His girlfriend dug around in her bag for tissue which he used to help me. I explained that I live nearby and was heading to the shop when some men decided they were jealous of my face and thought they'd mess it up. They insisted I notify the police. I didn't.

The truth is, I had been assaulted by my girlfriend in our kitchen. It wasn't the first time she'd punched me. It wasn't the first time I had lied about it. Later that night, it wouldn't be the first time I'd return home to her apology and give *her* a forgiving cuddle.

I can't speak for other men who keep loved ones and

strangers in the dark about the violence they experience; I can only assume we have similar reasons. I was sure it wouldn't happen again, at least, that's what she always said. I didn't want others to think badly of her; I loved her, after all! I'm known for articulating myself rather well, but it's difficult to make sense of that mishmash of feelings to help you understand. I guess I was protecting her and was also embarrassed to say that I had been hit and injured… by a girl. I am a man, after all!

As I received treatment on the street from an off-duty paramedic, my housemate returned home to find my girlfriend crying and blood all over the floor. He assumed I had hit her. She insisted he didn't phone the police, which he only agreed to when he realised she had perpetrated the violence. Apparently, that didn't warrant the notification of the police.

I'd like to say that if this happened in public, perhaps just one person might decide I need help; that someone might take me aside and ask if this happens behind closed doors. That someone might tell her how terrible that behaviour is. Truth be told, it happened in public a few times.

One night, in a club garden, she launched at me and punched my face. I didn't hit back, but pushed her away and she fell off her heels and onto the floor. The men and bouncers who had watched her attacking me suddenly burst into life, wrestled me to the wall and ordered me to wait for the police. After we broke up, she saw me in that same bar and, in front of at least thirty people, threw my own drink over me and extinguished her cigarette on my chest. She stomped away, enjoying the cheers and the drama, as I stood grimacing through the laughter of onlookers, wiping my face and telling my friend that I was 'fine'.

I don't share my experiences for sympathy or attention, but to raise the profile of one of the most significant inequalities suffered by men in our society today. The shocking fact is that my story, despite including blood, physical assault and the use of human flesh as an ashtray for an entertained crowd is, by no means, the most extreme example of female to male domestic abuse that I have witnessed or heard about. Domestic abuse is depicted as an exclusively male perpetrated crime. But what are the facts?

Since the 1970s, studies, for example by Murray Straus, have consistently demonstrated that both genders initiate intimate partner violence on a roughly equal level level, while some studies have even shown women are more likely to use more extreme violence against their partners. The Office for National Statistics currently reports that a third of domestic abuse victims are men. According to the statistics, women are more likely to suffer threats, stalking and serious sexual assault, while men are more likely to suffer financial and emotional abuse, and equally likely to suffer severe force, defined as "being kicked, hit, bitten, choked, strangled, threatened with a weapon, threats to kill, use of a weapon or some other kind of force." In a culture that encourages women to report abuse and provides support and refuge, women are also twice as likely to report abuse than men. Statistically, accounting for underreporting, not only are men equally victims of domestic abuse, but they are also equally likely to suffer severe violence, even in public.

Our tolerance of such an imbalance of power is actually a cultural norm: film and television have always considered it acceptable and even entertaining for a 'strong' woman to escalate a verbal argument with physical assault or throwing an object. Whether in dramatised fiction or the local pub, a female perpetrator of violence hitting a male is celebrated as assertive and dominant against someone 'who can take it' and 'probably deserved it.' Would any of us witness an offended man slap a woman, only to smirk, look the other way and whisper to a friend about how embarrassing that must be?

How can we change this harmful and sexist cultural perspective and ultimately work towards a society that supports victims of domestic abuse, regardless of their gender? At this stage, the onus is on us to challenge the male tendency to suffer silently and create confidence for victims to speak out, knowing they'll be heard and supported. To be abused is powerlessness, but it isn't weak. A man can take a punch, but shouldn't have to. To share stories of abuse and seek help may feel vulnerable… but that's okay. If we do not speak, we will not be heard.

Chris is a writer, musician and father of four.

How We Turn a Blind Eye to Male Victims of Sexual Exploitation

By Phil Mitchell

Boys and young men are often overlooked when it comes to sexual exploitation. People think they are tough and that they can look after themselves.

Services were originally set up for girls, not boys. Walls were painted pink and the imagery was of girls. This is not accessible to or inclusive of boys. Girls are being taught how to stay safe whilst boys are being taught something else. Then of course there's all of the gender stereotypes around masculinity, sexual orientation and asking for help.

People wrongly assume that this is an issue that affects girls, not boys but we need to be factual. Girls report more, girls disclose more and girls engage with services more – this does not mean it's happening less to boys. Also professionals generally look out for girls a lot more in comparison to boys.

A professional may see a 13-year-old girl in a situation with an older man and become concerned. If the same professional sees a 13-year-old boy with the same man, the level of concern is not always the same. This is something that needs to change. The only thing that is different is the gender – the risk is still the same, so why do some professionals respond in such a way that promotes inequality for boys?

Boys and young men who are gay or bisexual have additional vulnerabilities as they may feel isolated due to their sexual orientation which could lead them to seek older boyfriends as they don't know where to meet other LGBT people around their own age.

Boys and young men who are gay, bisexual or exploring their sexuality, are often given the message that they should be thinking about sex and that they should be having sex and this message is communicated to them much louder than it is to their heterosexual peers.

A 15-year-old heterosexual boy may attend a youth group where posters and images are age appropriate. A 15-year-old boy who is gay and attends an LGBT youth group may have access to sexualised magazines with half naked people on the cover and phone numbers of male sex workers at the back. This becomes further problematic if the boy thinks age does not matter and feels encouraged to seek an older sexual partner.

There is no doubt that both girls and boys who are sexually exploited need more help and support. In general, boys of all backgrounds who face sexual exploitation are less likely to receive help than girls, that's why it's essential that we make sure that services up and down the country are providing support that is accessible to and inclusive of boys.

Phil is Project Co-ordinator for the BLAST Project in Yorkshire, a leading UK project for male victims of sexual exploitation.

Yes, We Do Need to Talk About Men's Violence

By Ally Fogg

There is an exchange that plays out in the media on pretty much a daily basis. The moves have become so familiar we can see them performed almost as a ritual dance. In the aftermath of some tragic, violent incident – whether a mass shooting, a domestic homicide or a shocking sexual assault – a commentator with liberal or feminist leanings will describe the incident as an example of 'male violence' and, therefore, not just an isolated incident but part of a systematic pattern involving hundreds, thousands, millions of related incidents across the world each day.

There follows a storm of comments, social media updates and blogs as detractors – primarily but not exclusively male – throw up their digitised hands in horror and disgust. This is nothing to do with me! I've never killed anyone! Why are you blaming an entire gender for the crime of an individual?

The defensive reactions may be understandable, but are largely based on a misunderstanding. Saying that men have a problem with violence does not mean that all men are violent, any more than saying Britain has a problem with obesity means that all Britons are fat. In both examples, it means the phenomenon causes immense social harm and individual suffering, and occurs at levels far above those we should be willing to tolerate in a civilised society.

Yes, women can also be violent, especially towards intimate partners and family members. However in recent years the men's sector as a whole (and I include myself in that) has often become so fixated on demonstrating and documenting the extent of male victimisation at the hands of women that we may have lost sight of the bigger picture.

According to the UN's estimates, there are on average 450,000 homicides globally each year. Not only were 95% of the killers male, so too were 80% of the victims. In England and Wales, 800,000 adult men were injured in a violent attack in 2013 and around three quarters of perpetrators were not their female partners, but other men. On the other side of the coin, around 37,000 men are in prison today as a consequence of their own violent behaviour. To deny or turn our eyes from the extent of men's violence is to turn our backs on one of the most pressing and severe social and health issues facing men and boys across the world today.

Only once we acknowledge the scale of men's violence can we begin to ask why it occurs. I suspect many people are uncomfortable with the suggestion that there is something inherently violent to masculinity. What we might instead call 'male culture' colours our attitudes to work and to leisure, to lifestyles and relationships, even to how we communicate and interact. That culture has too often included attitudes towards violence that are directly implicated in too much death and injury.

How many of us grew up believing that to be a man demanded that we be 'tough' and 'hard', or in other words to be willing to endure and inflict violence? Such traits don't always come easy, and too many boys still have them literally beaten into us by peers or, tragically, parents and other adults. Research has consistently shown that where formal or informal physical punishment is used, boys are beaten more regularly and more forcefully than girls.

At the same time, psychologists have long known the rough recipe for a violent adult. According to one study by Murray Straus, a child who grows up in a family where the adults are violent to each other is almost three times as likely to display violent behaviour as others. Another study found that a child subjected to physical abuse who also witnesses violent behaviour at first hand, is between five and nine times as likely to become an abusive adult. It is true that not all violent adults lived through an especially violent childhood, and absolutely vital to understand that many, many people who experienced violence and abuse in childhood will never harm anyone in turn. Neither fact, however, should obscure the truth that violent adults – by which we most commonly mean violent men – are not born, they are made.

Nor does male violence exist in isolation from other male-specific issues. Only once we acknowledge and face up to the reality of male violence can we begin to unpick the complex relationship between men's emotional isolation and unaddressed mental health needs, our tendency to self-medicate or escape into excessive alcohol and drug use and from there, the intimate link between intoxication and violent behaviour.

It is not anti-man or misandrist to acknowledge that our society brutalises men and boys to a sufficient degree that some will become brutes. On the contrary, I would argue the misandrist position is to claim that men's violence is an inescapable law of nature, some relic of evolution or neurobiology. Testosterone does not breed violence, violence breeds violence, and the evidence, I am happy to say, is all around us. Current levels of violent crime remain distressing, but are a fraction of what they were 20 years ago. The vast majority of men are not violent and the numbers who are get smaller all the time.

As mentioned above, 800,000 men were wounded in violent attacks last year, but the same statistic in 1994/5 was 2.4 million. Domestic violence, as estimated by the Crime Survey of England and Wales, has dropped 78% over the same time frame. The same story is playing out across the developed world. Nor is it just the effect of increased prison populations keeping violent offenders out of harm's way. The number of children and young people entering the criminal justice system (ie being caught for the first time) is at its lowest since records began. Meanwhile the fastest growing section of the prison population over the past few years has been the over 65s.

The explanations for this phenomenal social change are hotly debated by criminologists but one thing is for sure, male biology has not evolved in a couple of decades. It is likely there are a variety of social and even environmental factors involved, I would suggest that it is no coincidence that the least violent generation of young men in living memory is the first to have been raised in the era of the rights of the child, in schools and homes that have increasingly eschewed violent punishments, with anti-bullying policies and where the social acceptability of violence of all sorts has been challenged and rejected as never before.

There is little doubt that men today are less violent, less aggressive, less militaristic than we have been at any time in living memory but there is still a long way to go. The journey will be driven not just by policy and politics but by the desire of all women, children and men to live in a safer, more peaceful world and the principal beneficiaries will be men ourselves.

Ally Fogg is one of the UK's leading media commentators on men's issues. You can follow his writing on gender at freethought blogs and find him writing in various publications especially The Guardian. *He's also a regular tweeter @AllyFogg*

What Can a Male Survivor of Sexual Violence Tell us about Human Kindness?

By Bob Balfour

Some days, I dream of a sexual violence/abuse victim-survivor activist protection programme, just like you see in those US films, with marshals flying in to rescue you from the bad guys – because you've done the right thing and challenged their power. When I watch those films and such an elite force goes into action to supply the witness with a new identity, I feel for both myself and the many others who've taken the decision, not only to disclose their childhood sexual abuse, but also very publicly to advocate and campaign for change in the ways we support its victims.

When you assertively challenge decision-makers and others who believe themselves to be professionals by asking them to step up to the plate and take a good, hard objective look at the evidence for change, the resistance you face as a survivor, male or female, is deep and well entrenched – especially when the call for change comes from male victims. You often find that people in power, in all its forms, resist considering paradigm shifts in intervention strategies for sexual violence/abuse crime victims. That resistance brings up unique issues for the male survivor, in my experience – fed by the taboos and myths which surround sexual violence/abuse.

My first sexually abusive experience occurred when I was aged six or seven. I now realize, aged 54, I've been searching since that moment for what it is to be male – in the sense of how maleness can help me to be more human than my abusers. In many ways, I've been investigating how to move beyond the constructions that build cloaks of gender – cloaks which are empowering of inequalities/abuse for both males and females. Does that make me a feminist? Perhaps – perhaps not… who knows? I prefer to think it makes me an explorer in humanness. The question is: what is humanness?

I'm a big fan of *Doctor Who* and have been for a very long time. In one episode, the Doctor had to face his deepest fear, and he initially explores everyone else's – even looking under the bed for that which stalks us in our dreams… fear itself. The legacy of sexual abuse in childhood is often a deep fear made up of so many dimensions even the Time Lords would struggle to unpack them easily.

In many ways the Doctor is looking to escape his fear and, given all the scandals and ongoing debate with the Home Office around who should chair a National Inquiry into sexual violence/abuse, it's tempting to wish for that elite unit tasked with rescuing activists, especially as you see the pressures building on survivors and the resulting infighting and projection. Anger will always find a target if denied a voice within a safe transparent space. Power is situational and, at all levels of engagement with sexual violence victim-survivors, informed kindness is needed to allow survivors the freedom to discover their own paths to voice and recovery.

As I watched the end of the episode 'Listen', my liking for Clara, the Doctor's companion, increased massively. We all need a Clara, I would suggest. I was lucky; mine was a First World War widow who lived on my Wallasey street in the 1960s. She made me bacon butties on a Victorian range every Sunday morning – she told me to always be kind. Her name was Mrs Rizten and I've always tried to do as she wisely advised and have never forgotten her.

Finally, in 'Listen', Clara finds a way to free the Doctor from his fear of his fear. She whispers, in his lonely and scared childhood ear, the following:

'If you're very wise and very strong, fear doesn't have to make you cruel or cowardly – fear can make you kind.'

I realized then I didn't need a rescue unit – I just need to remember those words, and Mrs Rizten, when my fear creeps out from under the bed and I feel the threat of becoming cruel or cowardly. All I need to do is remember to be kind, both to myself and others.

Soon I will need that kindness, as I will be in court to help bring a little more justice for my childhood peers and myself, hopefully. However, mostly I'll be there for all those who didn't make it to the point where they could find kindness from the fear. It would also seem the Doctor is a Time Lord 'care leaver' – thank you, Steven Moffat. A timely and very kind gift. The Doctor is now even more special for some lonely little boys and girls, frightened of what lies under the bed.

Hopefully, they will also find that kindness really

is the root of being human, regardless of gender, and that fear is a companion of us all indeed. In that lies our pathway to humanness and real justice against all abusers – it can 'bring you home', as Clara tells her Doctor. Brené Brown sums that up well and I suspect Mrs Rizten would approve:

'To be authentic, we must cultivate the courage to be imperfect – and vulnerable.'

Bob Balfour was sexually abused at the age of six. As an adult he has become one of the UK's leading advocates for male victims of sexual abuse after founding Survivors West Yorkshire in 2000. It operates a self-help website, www. matrix-west-yorkshire.info. He has worked with West Yorkshire's Police and Crime Commissioner to develop the capacity of third-sector agencies to bid for funding to deliver a region-wide service for adult male victims of sexual violence. He obtained a BSc Hons Psychology with Counselling at the age of 53.

GENDER POLITICS:

Time for a new conversation about men

So Why Do We Need to Talk About Men's Issues Anyway?

By Tim Samuels

When I dared to suggest that men should maybe get their own radio programme – just an hour a week, tucked away on a Sunday evening – it drew instant ridicule. For a tranche of female columnists, it was kneejerk stereotype-laden manna from heaven – to fill that week's column inches. *What on earth do blokes need to talk about? What do men have to moan about? They've already got football on the radio – what more do they want?* And so on…

That was five years ago now. Some sixty-plus years after *Woman's Hour* hit the airwaves, it's male counterpart was born – and *Men's Hour* survived its baptism of barbs. And as we enter series six, I dare venture that it feels like the wider climate has warmed in its attitudes to men, masculinity and male needs as something not to scoff at, but take seriously. The Southbank Centre has launched its Being A Man festival. *The Daily Telegraph* has a men's section. And *insideMAN* is the latest addition to a scene which rightly views the situation that men find themselves in today as more complex, nuanced and untethered than ever before.

For so long, the media and academia have viewed men as – in the observations of US writer Michael

Kimmel – 'the invisible gender'. So obvious is the enduring dominance of overall male power in society, that people forget to look at the experience of individual men. And through that prism of individual men, there is a far less cocksure dominance. Of course, that entitled unabashed confidence still exists amongst some men – perhaps in places like the lingering testosterone bastions of the City and Wall Street (though therapists dedicated to the Square Mile might beg to disagree). But it is a much rarer beast than in our ancestors' generations.

The evidence that men are struggling – or at least finding life less than straightforward – can be seen in the deeply troubling male mental health rates, the over-dominance of men in jails and sleeping rough on the streets, and the crisis in how to bring up boys. There's something about being a boy or man – and the expectations of masculinity – that's rubbing up against how modern society and the economy is operating.

Naturally, it's not all doom and gloom. The opportunities for a spot of hedonism are endless. Men have more freedom than ever before to be who they want to be – even if stalling social mobility might mean many will never get there. There's an emotional depth that fathers have with their children now that's thrown off any lingering stiff upper lip austerity. And perhaps – in the UK at least – this is the most liberating non-judgmental time to be a gay man in recent years?

As the old Facebook status update used to state, 'it's complicated'. Which means more than ever, men should be talking, sharing, dumping what's on their minds, never losing that protective dark sense of humour – and be given the space to flex our new-found emotional muscles without any daft barbs from columnists who've run out of anything useful to say.

Tim Samuels presents Men's Hour *on BBC radio 5 Live and is an award-winning TV documentary maker.*

Four Reasons Feminism is Alienating Teenage Boys

By Duncan Fisher

When I was asked to write one of the articles for the #100Voices4Men series I was chuffed. Then followed two months of absolute mental blankness. I watched with increasing panic as articles were published, reaching closer and closer to the 100 mark!

And then my daughter saved me. She reported that there had been a heated argument in an A-Level English class at her school about feminism. A week later, I had four 17-year-old boys from the English class sitting round our dining room table at home, and this article is about that conversation.

This is a group of young men keenly aware of the concerns of feminism, with a clear view of how the inequalities of concern to feminism are different in different environments. For example take the case of overt sexism in public places: there is none in the streets of our own small community where anonymity is no option, but in cities it is a different story. I described the harassment my youngest daughter has experienced while out running in Cardiff and at the time of our conversation, everyone on social media was debating the video in which activists captured on secret camera comments made to a woman as she walked around New York.

And then there is the internet, where sexualisation of women and girls and sexist trolling are rampant. We discussed their perceptions of equality in education. They see a very high level of equality in UK, but see a very different story in other countries and admire the campaigning of Malala Yousafzai.

They do not arrive at the same conclusion as the young man, Josh O'Brien, one of the other contributors to the series, who takes an anti-feminist view of gender politics. But despite this keen awareness, interest and concern, they don't engage in the debate on-line: "We never put our point of view across because there is too much hate".

So what's the story?

Four things cause real difficulty for these boys:

1. **When men who respect women are held responsible for the activities of men who behave horribly towards women.**

One of the young men said: "The story is that all men are dicks. We are being asked to sort these men out, but we are not responsible."

It called to my mind the recent complaint by British Muslims about being held to account for the actions of ISIS, leading to a great joke T-shirt: "I'm a Muslim and I am sorry for everything – in the past, present and future!"

Wagging the finger at all young men and saying

"repent!" is an incredibly ineffective recruitment strategy and alienates the men and boys equality work most needs.

2. When there is a lack of empathy for men who suffer

The young men are aware of those areas where men fare worse on average than women – relationships with their children after parental separation, access to mental health services, rates of suicide, death in war. A lack of empathy for these issues sends a dark signal. And in areas where the gender balance goes the other way, such as domestic violence or single parenting, why not open up our support equally to all according to need?

3. When statistics are abused

These young men (and, I am sure, countless young women) know that many of the statistics bandied about on social media are false – for example the one that says women earn 23% less than men, presented as if women are paid substantially less than men for the same work in a wide range of jobs. They know it cannot be true, because teachers in their school are paid equally irrespective of gender. But they have no doubt there are pay inequalities, though they don't have the resources to find out the truth of the matter, which is a painstaking and expert task.

They also know that if they do make any attempt at a contradiction, they will draw fire. So, even if they had all the figures, they have no real appetite for pointless rows. So the only option is to shut up. And so stupid statistics fly around on social media, giving people who want a fight a sense of justification for doing so; they are observed from the side lines by a large silent majority. Actual solutions, which depend on meticulous analysis of what is actually happening, get pushed into the background.

4. Fundamentalism on the internet

Social media spreads outrageous views far faster than reasoned arguments and the social media these boys see every day is awash with fundamentalist views that brook no contradiction. As the boys pointed out in particular, one video of little girls swearing and spouting ridiculous statistics (we all really hate this video) has gone hugely viral.

One boy said: "It keeps on appearing in my feed as the girls I am friends with share it", fuelling division between teenage boys and girls. The answer: keep a low profile. If you are targeted on-line, everyone can see. The same goes for large numbers of thoughtful teenage girls who would get fired at just as quickly.

And so the cause of gender inequality is deprived of its most valuable potential supporters on a grand scale. So I asked the boys, what conditions would have to apply to allow them to feel able to contribute to the debate about equality in the way they would like to?

They said they would need a safe place where they could feel confident they would not be shouted at and publicly humiliated; where their motives were not under immediate suspicion simply on account of their gender. They want protecting against fundamentalism by prominent and leading figures in the campaign for gender equality – people who can defend the sincerity of their interest and allow real discussion. They want to participate with girls and women of like mind.

Let us imagine for one instant what we could do if we could cultivate a strong and confident group of young women and men across the world committed to defending equality and having the tools to do so? A group of people ready to listen to the concerns of the other gender and to campaign together, modelling the kind of partnership between women and men that is predicated by equality?

What if all those watching the row about gender on the internet could also glimpse a place where an active, respectful and sincere campaign for equality was being conducted by women and men together?

This may be a pipedream. But let us remember: we will never end sexism and gender inequality without the help of boys and men – this has always been the case and will always be. And the first step is to listen to them without judgement, particularly those who are genuinely concerned and wish to participate.

As the boys left our house, they said how great it was to be able to have a sensible conversation about these things. I was struck that this was the first opportunity they had ever had to discuss gender equality without having to self-censor. That's a big problem.

Duncan Fisher OBE was one of the founders and CEO of the Fatherhood Institute and currently works to develop services for children that engage all the family.

A Fresh Analysis Requires New Alliances

By Jack O'Sullivan

To realise our full potential as men, we need to get the analysis and the alliances right. Feminism does men a favour by dismantling patriarchy, but it's up to us to challenge matriarchal values and finally end gender hierarchy.

First, the analysis. A big barrier to self-realisation is anything in our heads – or in other people's heads – which suggests that being male is a limitation rather than an aspiration. 'We can' should be reclaimed as the core of masculine identity. That means junking and challenging notions that we can't… express emotions, multi-task, care for children, care for ourselves and each other, listen, be valuable people even without a job… 'We can' does not claim innate ability. It establishes goals and entitlements. If we're not instantly good at something, it means that we seek help. We make sure that boys as well as girls emerge fully equipped for adulthood. We give men – as well as women – who might have missed out, both the opportunities and inspiration to catch up.

If that's the analysis, then we should make alliances with those who also say 'we can'. And we should challenge those who don't. Let's start with feminism. It has championed a philosophy that gender is no barrier to individual capacity. Women picked up this insight, historically considered to be a masculine paradigm. They ran with it and have travelled far together, outstripping men's sense of our own possibilities. Feminism should be our inspiration.

Patriarchy is our enemy because it confuses control over women and children with male self-realisation. We don't need to control others – we need to develop our own capacities. And patriarchy gets in our way because it dictates that only women do certain things. That stops us from doing them. Patriarchy says 'we can't' to men just as it tells women 'you must'.

Feminism has done us a favour in beginning to dismantle patriarchy. But it's left matriarchy for us to challenge. Matriarchal values – claiming that women are innately superior to men and that we are incompetent in key parts of the private and domestic arena – has messed up the heads of women and men. We have not supported equality in the public arena to then be policed and infantilised in our homes. Perhaps, in the old world, patriarchy and matriarchy somehow provided a balance, but both systems are out-dated as men and women reject gender-based power and its inevitable diminishing of the 'other' gender.

Then we have to talk about mending fractured relationships between different types of men. 'We can' requires mutual support. So, for starters, heterosexual men should dump their historic hostility to, and discomfort with, homosexuality. Straight men have a lot to learn from, and share with, our gay, bisexual and transgender counterparts, who have bravely and successfully said 'we can' about their contested identities.

And then there are fathers living with or separated from the mothers of their children. These fathers often act as strangers to each other. Men in 'intact' families provide little support for those fathering children after separation. Yet we're all saying, 'we can' be good parents. The power dynamics between fathers and mothers that become so obvious after separation are all present inside 'intact' relationships. They are just better hidden. We need to share our understanding of these dynamics.

Lastly, there's that word 'we'. Too many of us lack the will to collectivise in order to create a better world for everyone. Yet, individually, we are often unable to understand and tackle the cultural pressures that we face. Together, 'we can'.

Jack O'Sullivan is former Associate Editor and columnist at The Independent *and author of* 'He's Having a Baby', *the BBC Guide to Fatherhood. You can follow him on twitter* @ThinkOSullivan.

When I Talk About Men's Issues, My Wife Says I Sound Like a Cunt

By Darren Ball

After sharing a glass or few of chardonnay with my wife, she once told me something that surprised me; she said: *"When you talk about gender issues you sound like a cunt"*.

She then said something that surprised me even more: *"I told you that because I love you"*.

Okay, a little bit of work required on her bedside manner perhaps, but I sympathise with her. There exists online, a grotesque "manosphere" of angry individuals, claiming to talk for men and boys, but which is really a cover for deeply-held misogyny. As a *Guardian*-reading Stoke Newingtonite, I have a bit of an image problem.

I'm a socially-liberal atheist humanist, which is not at all contrary to feminism. I would be very happy to throw my weight behind feminism if only it campaigned on all gender issues in proportion to their relative significance: including problems faced by males. This is not like asking the Cat Protection League to rescue dogs: feminism is billed as being either a movement for gender equality, or a movement to end the patriarchy. Operating under either remit it should care for a raft of male issues that currently, as a movement, it ignores.

Men and boys have especially poor outcomes across a

139

range of areas that affect their physical, mental and spatial wellbeing – for example, homelessness, educational under-achievement, and men's role, status and place in the home, especially as adjudicated by the family courts. We know there would be a feminist shitstorm if the genders were reversed on *any* of the issues that disadvantage males. We know this partly because, for some issues in the past, the genders *were* reversed and there *was* a shitstorm (e.g. the education attainment gap), and partly because some societal ills have become women's issues despite the fact that they predominantly disadvantage men. Glaring examples of this are the Corston Report on vulnerable female inmates and a national strategy for women's mental health – men would equally benefit from similar strategies directed at them, but none exist despite men being the more affected gender both in terms of imprisonment and those who are at risk of suicide.

The inferior outcomes for men and boys in these areas and others are due to a combination of unequal concern and the patriarchal hierarchy, which requires a top and a *bottom* amongst men. Either way, true feminism should include these problems within its radius of concern. You'd have thought that somewhere on their spectrum between honour killings and the objectification of women in advertising, feminists would find a place for at least some issues where gender inequality/patriarchy negatively impacts upon males. But it seems they would rather talk about being patronised by washing powder commercials and mis-sold probiotic yoghurt than the disproportionately high male suicide rate and their sons' failed education.

If feminism won't campaign for gender inequalities that generate poor outcomes for males, then surely they won't mind if men form groups to help themselves? Wrong. If ambivalence towards males wasn't bad enough, some feminist activism directly briefs against vulnerable males:

1. Leveraging off men to promote women's interests.

When leveraging off men to promote women's interests, Newton's third law applies – that of equal and opposite forces. Women are pushed up by pushing men down.

As before with the Corston Report for vulnerable female prisoners (as an example), Corston uses traditional notions of male stoicism to argue that conditions that are too degrading for women are acceptable for men. Rather than dismantling the patriarchy, Corston (a feminist BTW) is cynically using it to advance the interests of the five per cent of prisoners who are female while overlooking atrocious conditions for 80,000 men. This is despite the fact we already imprison more men than virtually any other country in Western Europe (absolute numbers and per capita).

2. Actively denying that a vulnerable male group exists at all

Feminists have resisted male equivalents of female university groups, even though men are in the minority at many universities and are living in a very changed world to their fathers. With the most serious forms and consequences of mental health problems disproportionately affecting young men, feminists should be encouraging space for young men to reflect upon what it is to be a young man in a modern western society. However they resist attempts by men to help themselves, often dismissing their concerns as "*What about teh menz*" and smearing young men who attempt to organise discussion groups as misogynists.

Much worse however has been the feminist reaction to male victims of Domestic Violence (DV). Since the 1970s they have argued that DV is one of the ways in which men enforce the patriarchy, so it's a bit inconvenient for them if they have to acknowledge the existence of female perpetrators.

Feminist groups have gone to great lengths to convince us all that men who claim they've been abused by women either deserved it or are making exaggerated claims. Again the patriarchy, that feminists are avowed to dismantle, is used to advance their cause – we protect her and insist that he mans-up. This particularly virulent strain of feminist activism is actively vilifying an abused group with the full support of the liberal left and the conservative right.

I have also come to understand much more about the issues that affect women and girls. They *do* have a different path through life than men, meaning that they will face different challenges for which society should adjust. I don't understand people, especially young women, who argue that feminism has run its course and women now have full equality. What about:

- The full spectrum of sexual harassment (from Page 3 onwards)
- Under-representation of women in our supposedly representative parliamentary democracy and judiciary
- Women in public life judged by their looks regardless of their profession
- Discrimination against women in certain careers (usually those where competitive men want to joust with each other, from fields as diverse as investment banking to comedy)
- Online abuse of women by internet trolls – seemingly regardless of the subject

The reality is that sexism and patriarchy hurts both men and women, just differently.

If I have succeeded in convincing both sides of the debate that my wife's tipsy description of me required no further explanation: good. I haven't a side, I'm a humanist.

insideMAN *reader Darren Ball, is an individual with a keen interest in gender equality, who's trying to find balance and make sense of it all. He considers himself neither a feminist nor a men's rights activist. He's also a jolly nice, North London, liberal sort of chap who has a bad habit of bringing up men's issues at dinner parties.*

Why has everyone forgotten about male suffrage?

By Neil Lyndon

In an article for *The Telegraph*, arguing the case for a Minister for Men, Tim Samuels apologised for trespassing on feminism's most hallowed ground and said: "We men have not had to fight tooth and nail for our votes".

No doubt, everybody would go along with that. Everybody in this country is taught from infancy that the Suffragettes had to wrest votes for women from a brutal male establishment that was protecting the monopoly exercised by all men. My daughters learned that lesson at primary school before they had even been introduced to the cardinal beliefs of the world's leading religions.

As is so often the case with the feminist catechism however, everybody – including Mr Samuels – is looking at history with one eye. As a matter of fact, men did have to fight before all men could get the vote. And men's fight was not conducted in debating halls, demonstrations and salons, nor even from the relative safety of the prison cell. Before all British men were allowed to vote, poor young men had to be wounded in millions and to die in hundreds of thousands in a war from which all women were exempted solely by reason of their gender.

Mr Samuels was writing almost exactly on the 99th anniversary of the Military Service Act, under which every British man 18-41 was subject to conscription for the First World War. The actual wording of the Act was that every man of that age was "deemed to have enlisted".

Without any voice in the matter, therefore, every adult male was, from that moment, subject to military law. If he didn't go quietly (most did, of course) he could be forcibly removed from his home and transported to the front where, if he protested that he couldn't see any sense in that insane conflict, he might be subjected to a cursory field court martial and executed by firing squad.

Guess what? Most of the propertyless, working-class men who then suffered in the mud and were blown to shreds in some of the most gruesome carnage in human history had no right to vote. One of them was my own uncle Tom – a working-class private soldier conscripted at Christmas 1917 at the age of 18 and killed in battle at Cachy on the Somme on April 24, 1918. Nothing identifiable remained of him to bury.

Palmerston voiced the views of the ruling class in the nineteenth century when he wrote to Gladstone in 1864 and said: "I entirely deny that every sane and not disqualified man has a moral right to vote... What every man and woman too have a right to, is to be well governed and under just laws".

Before 1918, the vote was restricted not simply by sex but also by property qualifications. Roughly 60% of adult men were then entitled to vote. At the 1910 general election, 7,709,981 men were registered to vote. By the time of the 1918 general election there were 12,913,166 registered male electors in the United Kingdom. The 1918 Act is, rightly, most famous for having brought more than eight million women into the electorate; but, for the first time, it also enfranchised more than five million men over the age of 21 without regard to property or class.

Introducing the Bill, the Home Secretary George Cave said: "War by all classes of our countrymen has brought us nearer together, has opened men's eyes, and removed misunderstandings on all sides. It has made it, I think, impossible that ever again, at all events in the lifetime of the present generation, there should be a revival of the old class feeling which was responsible for so much, and, among other things, for the exclusion for a period, of so many of our population from the class of electors. I think I need say no more to justify this extension of the franchise."

The Bill was passed in the House of Commons by 385 votes in favour to 55 against. Not one woman was then sitting as an MP. The rotten repressive male Establishment voted 7-1 in favour of votes for some women (restricted at that point by age and property qualifications) and all men over the age of 21. In the 1928 Act, the franchise was extended to women on equal terms with men.

This mixed picture of the past is now almost entirely buried and forgotten. If you enter a Google search on "votes for men 1918", you might find a handful of entries in among hundreds of pages about women's suffrage. In my experience, not one person in 1,000 knows the full story.

For many years, as a kind of party trick, I have been asking people "how many men got the vote in the Representation of the People Act 1918?" I have never met anybody who knew the answer. When, some years ago, I asked this question of my oldest friend – Oxford graduate in PPE and one of the most completely scintillating intellects I have ever known – he indignantly replied "None, of course."

There is a reason why our view of this history is as biased, one-sided and prejudiced as the account of the Eighth Route Army that was taught to Chinese children under Mao.

The reason is that the whole truth is extremely inconvenient. It conflicts with the dominant feminist narrative which portrays women as the victims of repressive men, from whom liberation and progress had to be wrested by militant uprising. The true history of votes for women, however, is not a story of sex war but of a continuous progress of electoral reform over a century from 1832-1928 in which women's suffrage was only one element.

It is also true that, as a whole, that complete story does credit both to Britain and to men whose memory deserves our continuing honour, compassion and respect.

Neil Lyndon has been writing on gender issues for nearly 40 years. He is the author of No More Sex War *and the ebook,* Sexual Impolitics: Heresies on Sex, Gender and Feminism.

Forty Years in the Men's Movement

By Paul Morrison

I have been in or running men's groups now for forty of my nearly seventy years. They have been a rich arena of support, warmth and understanding, a place to be challenged lovingly, a place to explore and re-shape my sense of myself as a man and as a human being. Now, as I watch myself grow older with other men who are also growing older, life continues to throw up its challenges, new layers of vulnerability are exposed. There is no shortage of material for discussion and exploration, no lack of questions to be answered, in these our mature years.

We began meeting in response to the women close to us who were embracing feminism – the second wave – in the early seventies. Women were demanding equality, demanding to be taken seriously in the workplace, challenging the widespread assumptions I had grown up with: men as providers, breadwinners; women as domestic labourers and child-rearers; men as rational; women as emotional; men as powerful in the world; women as keepers of the home; women as passive and as sexual objects; men as active and sexual drivers.

The new women historians were telling us that this gender division of labour wasn't an inevitable outcome of biological difference. It hadn't always been this way.

Even during the war recently fought, women had taken on all kinds of roles for which they had previously been deemed unfit.

We saw the justice of the women's movement: it was incontrovertible that the wider world we lived in was run for the most part by men, and that women's countervailing authority in the arenas of family and childcare was largely demeaned, patronised and undervalued, as was emotionality itself. Some of us were confused, feeling at times that we carried the sins – and the privileges – of millennia of patriarchy on our shoulders. At the same time we wanted to resist that guilt, to start again from where we were, and find a way to be as men that acknowledged the history and supported the fight for equality, but didn't mean we had to be forever ashamed of our man-ness.

To begin to look at this, we needed to talk to one another. We needed the support of other men. We borrowed the model of consciousness-raising from feminism, and formed a group. It was an experiment. It didn't have a label or an ideology, It was men talking to one another about their hopes and fears.

To start with these conversations carried a sense of our identities being under threat. Before long it grew into a positive sense of wanting to re-shape ourselves and our lives. We liked being together. We liked talking together. We discovered that it was safe to share our vulnerability with one another, when so much male upbringing had been supposedly about bullying, competing and getting one over on one another. What had been once defensive became an exciting and deeply meaningful re-ordering of priorities. Feminism instead of being a threat became an opportunity: to move out of rigidly prescribed masculine roles and allow ourselves more emotional openness; to seek closer and more engaged relationships with our children; to be truly equal in our relationships with our partners.

Some of us committed ourselves to share childcare and housework. Amid the joy and pride in discovering that we indeed had the capacity for care and nurture, we could at times find ourselves lonely and isolated: the only man in the park with a pushchair; the only guy among the women in the playgroup. We learnt to use the men's group for support rather than relying always on the women in our lives to emotionally prop us up. Some of us explored the burgeoning humanistic psychotherapy movement, and introduced some of that therapy awareness into the men's group.

We attended and helped to organise men's conferences bringing together the men's groups that were emerging nationally. We founded and produced a magazine, *Achilles Heel*, intended as a kind of cousin to *Spare Rib*, which brought in other men and gave a voice to the burgeoning movement, and to the re-thinking of masculinity that went with it. We organised residential weeks for men and children. We attended demonstrations, supporting for example a woman's right to choose. We founded a men's centre in a condemned building. We held men's days, jointly with gay men.

Going public felt scary, a kind of coming out. The press coined the term 'new man', something we never claimed for ourselves, wanting not to separate ourselves and to see the humanity in all men. Having invented the term, the press then used it to derogate and patronise us. Some women in the broader feminist movement were hostile, seeing us as using the men's movement to reclaim their power. Some gay men were also angry at what they saw as an attempt by heterosexual men to claim victim status. But many understood what we were about and were supportive.

We were cautious about building a national organisation. We didn't want to set up yet another hierarchical structure with middle class white men at the top. Men's task at that time was to go inside and into the family; it was women who were staking a claim for access to the wider world.

In the years since, I have watched many of the skilled jobs that sustained the industrial trade unions be eviscerated, and with them the role of men as sole or main breadwinner. I have seen many men whose dignity and self-respect depended on those jobs become stranded and embittered. Rates of male suicide and mental breakdown rose as a result, many men lacking the resources, internal and external, to socialise their hurt and anger.

I have watched the growth of 'lad-ism' as the dominant male culture, retaining many of the cultural props of the older culture – pubs and clubs, gambling, watching sport, and a kind of exaggerated sexism with irony – but without the sense of duty and responsibility that the role of bread-winner offered and could take pride in. It has felt to me like a faux-identity, transitional, and ultimately a dead end. It reached its apogee in the banks and in the City, and I would hope it is finally losing its thrall.

I have watched the emergence of some brave men's

campaigns against the out-dated prevailing wisdoms of the divorce and family courts that men are second-rate parents, at best an optional extra, and should stick to being providers. They were fighting sexist institutions that appeared to favour individual women, but in the long run trapped them in their role. So these campaigns needed to set a careful tone. Sometimes they suffered from coming across as anti-feminist or even misogynist, when to my mind they were questioning the same structures that we were.

I have seen role models for men in the mainstream change enormously. Men are expected now to attend births, change nappies, and be engaged with children in a way previously unacknowledged or unthinkable. There is more tolerance of men's emotional expression. Male culture is more open, more inclusive of difference. There's currently a mini-explosion of 'men's work' on a whole range of issues: suicide; men's health; gang culture; AIDs among third world men; mentoring and role models for boys; rites of passage for older men; post-natal depression; aging. To grow up as a man in the UK today means hugely different challenges and choices to those we inherited growing up in the fifties.

I feel proud and blessed to have lived this journey; to have played a part in opening up these questions. We have made a start. We have a way to go.

Paul Morrison is a film maker and psychotherapist, and was a leading figure in the anti-sexist men's movement of the 1970s and early 1980s.

My 12-Point Plan to Fight for Equality for Men and Boys

By Mark Brooks

Everyone who works in the "men's sector" knows there are many areas of life where men and boys face inequality – health, education, homelessness, criminal justice sentencing, suicide rates, crime and violence, to name but a few.

Yet the quest to make our voice heard seems impossible at times. It's almost as if male inequality is invisible and when it is known, those with power do little or nothing to address or recognise it.

From government gender equality surveys, in which one gender seems not to be included, to party political conferences, where fringe meetings routinely tackle female-related issues (which is not a problem), but ignore issues that affect men.

There is no public voice on male victims. The political class are not interested, so we have to speak up ourselves.

But none of us should rely on others to make the case, to make a noise and create the solutions we have to do it ourselves. This applies to all men and women who are concerned with the issues that face men and boys, for whatever reason. Those of us who work for men's charities must help and encourage others to speak out.

Take three issues (of many) that affect men and boys from cradle to the grave:

Education: Boys continue to fall way behind girls at every level of education – in 2014 boys were 8.8 percentage points behind girls at GCSE and over a third more girls applied for a place at university than boys. On the latter, we can already see the outcome when it comes to the numbers entering the professions.

But who in the government or the education establishment is actually seriously talking about it or doing anything of substance and scale to tackle it?

Homelessness: No one debates or discusses homelessness in a way that specifically acknowledges it is primarily a male issue, despite the fact Crisis say 84% of the hidden homeless are men and street surveys show 9 out of 10 people sleeping rough are male. Who is providing the solution to why men are more likely to be homeless than women and what are the solutions for both genders? Is homelessness not on the agenda because it is a male issue?

Suicide: Perhaps the most harrowing issue of all is suicide. We know that 78% of all suicides are male with 4,861 men committing suicide in 2013. Yet there is political silence on this crisis. Male suicide prevention charity, CALM, are doing a great job of raising awareness of the issue, but it is about time the government listened more. Why is it not at the top of the political agenda?

So what to do? Outlined below is a brief 12-point plan – which I outlined at the National Men and Boys conference in 2012. More detail is needed of course, but it is a start and I hope to do more work on it over the next year. In case much of it seems like I'm teaching grannies to suck eggs, please forgive me.

1. **Provide and create solutions:** We can't be just 'keyboard warriors' and campaigners, we have to set up charities and organisations that provide services to support men and boys. To solve the need for support services ourselves, we have to campaign, complain and create. Lead by example. Don't rely on others. The brilliant Working With Men is an example to us all.

2. **Use the language of the public sector**: Like any institution it has its own language and codes. To get inside the tent, we need to use the language of the public sector and use it to our advantage by showing that services need to be provided for men and boys. It then becomes even more powerful. The term 'equality' and 'based on need' are such powerful tools. It is why I refer to the work we do as being equality and needs based, not rights based.

3. **Strike the right tone**: Sadly people only take in 20% of what you say, but 80% of how you say it. As someone from Sahf Eest Lahndan I understand it acutely. And tone is important – be positive, be charming and rightly be supportive of the good work that supports women and girls. Confrontation only works in certain rare circumstances.

4. **Include women in the solutions, stories and examples**: The gender of the people who advocate for men and boys should not matter, but it does. Fighting for equality, recognition and services for men and boys in a 'sector' that is dominated by women and is overwhelmingly focussed on women (the only focus on men is often because 'men are the problem'), means having female voices advocating for men and boys is very powerful. It often produces a 'double take reaction' and even our charity manager has been questioned about why she is involved at the ManKind Initiative. Erin Pizzey, Jane Powell and Karen Woodall, are brilliant examples of women advocating for men.

    On the public story front, also use examples which will resonate with the sectors' ears. As part of my domestic abuse narrative I always try to include mothers and sisters of male victims, and of course, a victim's daughters.

5. **Case studies:** As a PR man, facts and campaign slogans are one thing, but nothing brings a story or campaign to life better than real-life examples. They are also brilliant for challenging those who oppose support for what you are campaigning for, especially if there is a female element to the case study. For example, if I get challenged about the importance of male victims of domestic violence, I could point people to the story in which a woman was jailed for eight years after attacking her boyfriend with a

hammer and broken bottle, in what police described as 'one of the worst' cases of domestic violence they had seen.

6. **Use the laws we have**: This could be a book in itself, but there are two vital pieces of legislation in the equality campaigner's toolkit.

   The first is the Equality Act 2010 which in a nutshell means that all public bodies have to end discrimination against those with protected characteristics (gender being one) and how different people will be affected by their activities. The Act helps them to deliver policies and services to meet the needs of those with protected characteristics. This means, under the Public Sector Equality Duty which forms part of this law, councils, police forces, the health service etc. have to ensure they support men and boys not only in a general sense but also in a specific sense if there is a male-centric need. For example, ensuring domestic abuse services support men as well as women, or the local health service runs campaigns about prostate cancer. Quote this law and the Duty at every opportunity when fighting for services and recognition.

   The second piece is the Freedom of Information Act 2000 which is more of a tool to use for the above. This act means you can ask public bodies for statistics, information and research (and a whole lot more) to support your cause. We at ManKind use it to obtain the number of male victims reporting to different police forces each year and also used it to find out who had won funding from the Home Office for male domestic abuse services – and also who didn't win and why they didn't.

Just on facts and FOI, the more local the information the better and do not ask for too much detail because your request can be refused for being too costly.

7. **Do not get dragged into debates about feminism**: Another chapter for another book, but there are two reasons why this is important. Firstly, you are fighting for something tangible, a service or a campaign, you are not fighting against what is essentially a concept/belief system. Secondly, you will get distracted, getting taken down blind alleys and run the risk of alienating people who could be, or are, allies. Do not be defined by other people's belief systems, be defined by the fact that you want to support men and boys.

8. **Support each other**: Collaboration between charities supporting men in my mind is weak. It is primarily driven by the fact we are all so underfunded our focus is on survival and service provision (In November 2014, Refuge advertised for a woman-only senior communications manager whose salary was higher than the Mankind Initiative's previous year's income), but also some is territorial. I don't understand the latter but we do need to collaborate. A good example is on International Men's Day, for the second year running I have contacted men's

organisations to see if they will "lend us their logo" so we can say they support the aims of International Men's Day – only a few have and some significant charities (who will be nameless) have not. Why?

So we need to speak to each other more, form joint campaigns/services and also provide a listening and helpful ear. We are all in it together.

9. **Reverse the genders:** This is a classic tactic that must be used shamelessly and one advocated powerfully in Neil Lyndon's seminal No More Sex War. Reversing the genders brings out in an understandable fashion the barriers, hypocrisy and discrimination men and boys face and the need for support and services for them – boys dying because of botched circumcisions is one example. Also it can be used to devastating effect as a campaign tool.

10. **Keep calm, do not show frustration and do not be provoked by men-haters:** We know we feel we are pushing water uphill and there are those who want us to fail – some for ideological reasons, some because they fear funding being switched and some simply because they don't like men. Rise above it.

11. **Never advocate for funding to be cut from women's services and given to men**: This is from both a moral and practical perspective. If we believe in equality of support for those in need, which is why we are campaigners and service providers, then morally because women do have problems to fix,

we shouldn't want to see funding switched. If you advocate that position, then no matter what you say, no one will be listening and rightly so. It is also always worth setting that context for this upfront – it clears the air and sets a reassuring framework for you to work within.

12. **Do not sell out – for money, influence or anything**: So you get the government or state funding, you start to grow your services, you get comfortable and then an issue breaks or you see that something is not working. Your natural instinct is to speak out on behalf of your beneficiaries but you know it may damage your relationship with your funders. If you hesitate, blink or stay silent – you have sold out. Don't!

Mark Brooks is Chair of The ManKind Initiative, a charity that helps and advocates for male victims of domestic violence. You can follow them on twitter @ManKindInit.

MEN'S LIFE EXPERIENCES:

Being a man

The Moment We All Dread, Yet Secretly Long For: Being Forced to Leave a Job You Hate

By Karl Coppack

Looking back, the moment I was called into a meeting with one of our Directors, I knew the writing was on the wall. Ordinarily, this would never have happened as she was way up the ladder to deal with the likes of me but, as our buffer was on holiday, she stepped in. She wanted 'to see how I was getting on', which is probably the last thing she wanted to know, really. I'd be surprised if my wellbeing ranked highly on her list of concerns. Instead, we played the game of rictus smiles and half-hearted laughs as we filled in our time before the real business was addressed. Then it came. I was asked if I was 'happy'. That was a pretty deep question to be asked at any time and for a second I considered a pathos dipped speech about my lack of football career, how it seemed that I was constantly overlooked by Thandie Newton and how Piers Morgan drove me to murderous thoughts but I knew what she meant. Was I happy here?

Well, no.

Really, no.

If anything it was a rhetorical question. What she really meant was that she was unhappy. Unhappy with me.

I knew that this chat, this 'catch up' was coming. A day earlier she'd commented that the page of data I had on my screen had been there untouched for hours and thereby insinuated that I had done little work to push it along. She didn't realise that the monitor was a split screen and my laptop was working away below, unseen to the untrained eye. I had been working, albeit with a sigh as another day became another week became another year became a lost life.

She knew we were about to go our separate ways. It had been hinted at for weeks and, although they wouldn't say it, my departure would be welcomed and an ambitious young buck, who had never heard of The Smiths, would soon settle into my chair. I was ready for this and had plans but I wasn't ready to announce them just yet. I wanted to do it when it suited me. I could have stonewalled her and added to the false *bonhomie* with grins and shrugs of my own but I was tired. Tired of the whole futile exercise. I didn't want to play this game anymore. It had long since bored me to perdition and beyond. I leapt in and made my announcement. A sentence later I was waving goodbye to a twenty-year media sales career.

This was no snap decision. The writing on the wall was there for all to see and it was a shame in some ways. I'd enjoyed some of my time there – strapped to a phone or slogging up and down motorways but over the years the prospect of more empty time manacled to that desk had dampened any remaining enthusiasm. I worked in trade exhibitions and only six months earlier had worked on an event with which I had a passion, but thanks to a few internal changes I was placed on a show which held absolutely no interest – literally none at all. I should have left then but the commission was good. After a while that wasn't enough, as even the added incentive of money evaporates after a while. I was aware that time was nudging me in the ribs. Time for a change.

But what change? The trouble was that I was well aware of what I didn't want but when it came to the next step I was at a total loss. What I didn't want was clear. I didn't want another sales target. I didn't want to look elated when the company did well. I didn't want to attend another sales conference and sit through high-octane lectures about 'hitting our numbers'. I didn't want that. My applause at those events was soulless. I felt like the most downtrodden North Korean citizen emptily saluting a leader. I was a corporate fraud and they knew it.

I'm 46 in November. Most of the people my age are managers as I was years earlier. However, I had long decided that the managerial cloak wasn't for me. I wasn't bothered if people were late. I didn't care if they left a bit early. I had no interest in control and discipline. This, apparently, was not the right attitude.

There were other factors too. I didn't fit into a team mentality. See, I can't whoop. No. I can't high five. I can't 'smash it' when 'achieve' will do. I can't 'do drinks' – I go to the pub. I can't fake love for an overlord who doesn't know my name. I can't sound a horn when I've sold something. I like to go to work, do my bit, and then go home. I'm not much of a mixer. Oh, I had mates there but things seldom went out of office hours. The company ran social events so we could all 'bond'. I went to one – a quiz night. I went because I thought I could win. I did. Go me. I never went again.

You'd think my age might be a reason for this mealy-mouthed approach. I was older than most people in this thriving young enterprise but that wasn't the case. Truth is, I've always been like this. I wasn't critical of such people or ideals – there were some lovely and glorious people there whom I openly adore. It's just that I didn't care. I couldn't fake an interest in the company's common good. To their credit, my lack of engagement wasn't really deemed a problem. I made a great deal of money for a great many people and was well paid for it with a car thrown in. We both knew what we were doing. As Senator Pat Geary tells Michael Corleone in *The Godfather: Part Two*, we were both part of the same conspiracy.

You spend so much of your life at work. You see your loved ones for a few hours a day and a bunch of strangers for twice as long. Not right, is it? There's nothing you can do about it – we all have to work after all but we do get a say in what we want to do. We forget that from time to time – the concept of choice and change. It took me two decades to move from one life to a happier one. But which happier one? Liverpool, Thandie Newton and Piers were not playing ball.

There was one thing I wanted to do but it seemed a bit far-fetched.

Six years ago, a few mates and I raised some cash for a former footballer. We worked hard, had a laugh and managed to help one of our heroes. It took us a year before we reached our target and we soon returned

166

to our normal, everyday lives. Something changed though. It lit a fire, or rather a small smouldering ember, under me as I can honestly say that I achieved more job satisfaction from those few months than in my entire working life. I loved fundraising. I loved the feeling that I'd done something to improve someone else's life. I never really got that with exhibition sales. I still went to my normal job though and wasted more years. It really was a nice car.

During the odd sulk at work I'd edit my CV and apply for a few charity jobs. I even managed the odd interview but my lack of experience in that world went against me. Time and again I would reach the latter stages only to fall at the last hurdle. Finally, a week before this meeting, someone took a chance and opened up a fresh challenge. The change had finally been made. It just took a firm decision, some not-entirely subtle persuasion from my former charges and a kind-hearted fundraising director.

Of course, this is just me. It could go the other way. There may be hundreds of you who can no longer bear the public sector and crave breakfast meetings and the new argot that goes with media sales – from high value donors to high fives, as it were – but this is my tale and you'll have to get your own if you don't like it. The point is, change is usually an option.

We can't all walk into our ideal jobs, There are restrictions on us all, after all – wages, opportunity etc. but it's always worth remembering that you never HAVE to work anywhere where you're not happy. You can leave. You can change course. You don't have to take it. You can at least look and ask. That costs nothing.

I've been in my current role for two months and I love it. I've no idea what the next day will bring but I no longer pray for Friday. I'd have never thought that possible. Sure, there'll be frustrating times to come but I'll never forget the despondency that led me there in the first place and I can't allow myself to go back to that. I left in July with four years on the clock. There was to be no speech, no card, no leaving do and no gift. They didn't give a toss. It appals me that I once did.

But, no regrets. We're only here for a short time so why waste it on nothing? I walked out a little angry and upset at the indifference but those days are gone now. We must make up for the past by securing the future. Goals are important even if it's for a slight change. If you're not cut out for something then at least try to move on. There's little sense in living a brief life with no joy. I'm no example of that – I took too long – but as Morrissey once said 'There is another world. There is a better world. There must be.'

He's right too.

I'm just waiting for Thandie Newton now.

Karl is a former writer for Through The Wind and Rain *and a whole host of others who are desperate for copy. Troubled with the modern world, grimaces at ball-playing centre halves and frowns at fancy-dan back heels. Apt to talk about the magnificence of Ray Kennedy wherever possible.*

Karl's debut novel, And What Do You Do? *is available on Kindle download (not about footy). To check out more of his writing visit* The Anfield Wrap *and follow him on Twitter @thecenci*

The Day I Realised I'd Married My Wife into a Lifetime of Racism

By Kenny Mammarella-D'Cruz

'At least I'm not a nigger and I work for a living!' That was my Italian wife's first real racist 'attack', behind my back, from the car rental man in a deserted Santorini Airport as we arrived around midnight for our honeymoon. Here is what I learned from this.

1. **I will not allow my wife to be abused, threatened or insulted.** As a child I allowed racial abuse to cut me, break my spirit, embarrass me – and I let it go. I was told that if the people of the town that we had moved to (as Goan, Ugandan refugees) didn't like

us, then 'we'd have to move and we have nowhere else to go'. So best turn the other cheek, like a good Catholic boy, and understand their need to try out some of the hilarious racist material that was commonplace in '70s media, and accept that those who felt they were the lowest in society might need to pass abuse on down the pecking order in order to feel better about themselves.

2. **I can't truly protect my wife**, or anyone else from abuse, pain, fear, the things that I don't wish them to feel. I'm an old-fashioned man who likes to protect and provide. I'm a modern-day man who shows up with an open heart. I cried in the bathroom as my wife slept in our honeymoon bed, realising that I'd married her into a life of racism and potential danger. I don't bottle things up as much as I used to, I now have more space for love.

3. **I will stand up for my wife, myself and what I believe is right, meeting what I believe needs changing head-on.** Neither my wife or I were brought up in families who quite knew how to stand up for ourselves and it has cost us all dearly. This is where our limiting family habits stops and the family curse is broken. So I didn't make my wife's backhanded racist abuse okay by brushing it under the carpet, as some suggested.

My wife and I don't want the man punished, sacked or harmed in any way. We want him to be accountable for what he said and educated around the consequences of bullying, abuse, and what might be best said out of the public ear. The fact that he said this to my wife, behind my back, felt to me like an adult who would physically abuse someone vulnerable like a child or an elder without leaving marks as evidence.

4. **In some cultures use of 'the n word' is still acceptable.** All it took in school was for someone to call me a nigger and I was shut up in an instant with no comeback. For some it was hilarious! So I played small, played safe and lived in fear of it, laughing it off the few times it pierced my spirit.

    I was astounded when the rental firm initially said that my wife must have misheard and he might have said: 'At least I'm not a 'beggar'. Then they came back with "he was referring to himself 'working like a nigger'."

5. **The nicest people can have bad days, leaky shadows, snap at the final straw and lose control as 'the red mist' takes over.** I am sure that 'Grandpa' who 'served' us is a lovely old man who delights at spreading holiday happiness and joy. He badgered my wife for an extra 50 euros as she tried to explain that she'd paid an excess fee before boarding the plane. He wanted his extra money and I stopped his insistence asking "Are you calling my wife a liar?" and that's when the red mist fell. For an eternity we fiercely stared each other out to near breaking point. I know, from childhood experience, how the red mist can take a person over.

171

6. **I learned to step back, allow breathing space and put someone else's needs before my fight for justice.** He finally showed us a document with 25 euros in red, which was true. I thought it best for me to step back and let my wife deal with the admin avoiding things turning nasty. He asked my wife "Did I call you a liar? At least I'm not a nigger and I work for a living!" Shocking and scary. She didn't tell me what he'd said until we were in the car. I knew she wanted to just leave and feel safe again.

7. **People, corporations, bullies, etc. will get away with whatever they can without admitting liability.** I wonder whether the car rental firm were obliged to avoid admitting what happened and therefore any liability? We never got to hear Grandpa's version of what happened and feel like we've been sent from pillar to post by the firm without anyone really taking this on and dealing with it, until my Rottweiler persistence prevailed ten weeks later, when our car hire fee was refunded 'as a gesture of good will'. This incident took over our honeymoon, my 50th birthday celebrations, our thoughts and emotions. My wife spent our honeymoon dreading coming face-to-face with her abuser again. I don't feel the good will.

8. **My pain is my choice and it's something that others might find uncomfortable.** As do I, as I learn and grow from it. I wanted to sit in the reality of what had ruined our feelings of safety in this foreign country, even though other people were very

nice to us in Santorini. Were they just pretending? What were they really thinking? Are my wife and I safe? I was grateful for this fearful space that my new wife and I could get real in, rather than brush under the carpet to fester and follow us around, occasionally rearing its ugly head for us to look in the eye and eventually face. We sat with this with gratitude that it had come up now, as we look to buy our first property together, to be aware of neighbours and neighbourhoods. I felt that if we didn't take the opportunity to lay a boundary on how we will be treated now, then we will surely have to do it later. So as we laid the boundary and have set ourselves up for a life of love and safety.

9. **The sooner pain is named, the sooner pain can be released.** Half way through my email exchanges with the firm, my wife took over, as she was ready to deal with it herself: after all the offending words were said to her while she was alone and vulnerable. This honeymoon parasite was released as she named it, allowing the story to separate from us.

    I always tell the men in my men's groups and my private clients that the way I organize my priorities is to do whatever relieves the most pressure first. Easy to say, but that might be where the most fear, pain, avoidance, trauma or even liberation lies. Who would I be without my story? My wife needed her time to be ready to write it down and out of her and move things on, as I am doing now. When it's time – it's time. What a relief!

10. I learned that the experiences and stories from my past can still haunt me, if the nerve is touched. As I name them, l let them go and make space for more goodness in my life. I was raised in a small, Catholic, Portuguese-influenced bubble that was happily lost in time until Idi Amin so shockingly popped it. I've probably been called a nigger more than I've been called anything else. This is despite the fact for some people I'm 'officially' not black enough to call myself black, and I was certainly not black enough for Idi Amin!

After the refugee camps we were brought up in a small town in West Wales with wonderful neighbours in a generally accepting community – we were the only coloured family there for a long time. We fled Amin's Secret Service losing everything, including my father for nine months.

One day a man showed up at our house with a load of furniture, old toys, books, all sorts of things including a very old set of encyclopaedias, where I found a section on how black natives were more like animals than civilized white people and how they should be treated as a result. I wondered what the people in our community really thought about us. Some local children thought that my father might eat them if they behaved badly, others thought we were 'red Indians' and searched behind and under our furniture for hidden bows and arrows.

I remember Alex Haley's book *Roots* taking the screens by storm in the 1970s and I could see the noose hanging from the tree in my mind's eye as I cried in our bathroom in Greece. (Totally illogical, but try explaining that to the traumatised little boy inside of me.) That hanging noose has always scared me and I remember not telling my family about what I saw in the encyclopaedia and fretting about how I would protect them if the locals got ideas and turned on us. How will I protect my wife?

I was physically attacked in the changing rooms on my first day of secondary school and another boy – who was used to fighting and didn't risk expulsion from the community – took the attacker on and nothing more was said of it by the teachers or other kids. Changing rooms were humiliating and I felt like Joseph Merrick 'The Elephant Man' because of distant examination and perfectly innocent, though embarrassing questioning.

I missed out on normal boyhood fun and games. I've caught up in my later years and I've turned into the healthy, self-respecting man that I feel that I now am, happily married and loving my London life, transforming the shadows of my psyche into the gold of walking a conscious path, with my wife by my side. Shame it cost us our honeymoon, but in some strange way perhaps it was a good thing we rented that car.

Kenny Mammarella-D'Cruz is a personal development consultant who provides men with the tools they need to transform their lives and businesses. Known as "The Man Whisperer" he has worked with hundreds of men through his MenSpeak men's groups and in his work with private clients, couples and businesses. Kenny is regularly featured in the national media talking about the challenges men face. To learn more about Kenny's work, visit his website www.kennydcruz.com

What's it Like for Dads who Experience the Loss of a Child Through Miscarriage?

By Al Ferguson

Miscarriage is a mysterious and devastating thing. I don't think dads talk about their experience of miscarriage enough, and they should. They should because it's real, it's very common and it helps to talk about it. Here is the story of this Dad's miscarriage.

My wife and I had planned to get pregnant and could not have been happier when we saw the two blue lines. But during week six the storm began when my wife found a small amount of blood. We quickly Googled and found out about spotting common, perfectly-normal bleeding during early pregnancy. We put it down to this, but the doctor still booked an appointment at the emergency scan department of the hospital.

This was a weird place! We were sitting in a corridor, opposite the sonographer's room. Women and couples go into the room with an anxious look on their face and come out either crying or gleefully holding a baby scan picture. We sat there and wondered our fate.

Overjoyed or distraught? We ended up feeling neither. The sonographer examined, and came to the conclusion that it was too early to tell, booking us in for another emergency scan in two weeks' time. That way the heartbeat would definitely be seen. (Or not.)

This time the foetus had grown but there was still no visible heartbeat. No-one could explain it and no-one could confirm viability either way. We epitomised the saying, "left hanging". We lived the following weeks on edge, anxious, worried and pensive. All the while this was happening we were planning our wedding for the end of the summer.

What should have been an exciting time of preparations was overcast by a huge cloud of uncertainty and potential devastation. Just before our pre-wedding honeymoon was our third scan… Still no heartbeat but more growth! The doctor said, because of the growth, she couldn't definitively say to us that we would lose the baby. Instead she gave a 95% chance of miscarriage at any point. So what should we do? Miss our holiday and lose the money, or go and risk it? We decided to go, but all the while our thoughts were elsewhere.

On our return, general wedding stress levels were non-existent. The Tuesday before the wedding saw us, yet again, in the emergency scan waiting room for a fourth scan. We hid ourselves from the others, knowing that it would more than likely be bad news. This time, there was still no heartbeat but also no growth. We were told it was just a matter of time before the body rejected the unviable foetus and the miscarriage began. We had two options:

1) Let the miscarriage happen naturally over the wedding, or:

2) Opt for the SMM (Surgical Management of Miscarriage) and cancel the wedding?

Ever been between a rock and a hard place? We decided to crack on with the wedding and if the miscarriage started, we'd cross that bridge as and when. It put everything into perspective. It helped us focus on us, and ironically, in amongst the sadness, we had never been so close. We got married with such an intimacy between us.

Three days after the wedding the miscarriage started. It began as a pain in the stomach. She knew it was happening, so we called for our fifth emergency appointment. The bleeding was constant and she had continuous pain. What could I do to make it better? The helpless feeling of inadequacy was fraught and very real.

Seven weeks of uncertainty, hope and despair had come to an end. We booked in for an emergency SMM. We arrived at the hospital and got prepped for the procedure. It was gut-wrenching and as they wheeled my wife out of the room I felt like my heart was being pulled out on a trolley too. I couldn't be with her when she was terrified, I wanted to comfort her, hold her hand and be there for her. Instead, I was in a cold room with just my thoughts as company.

Following the procedure it was so hard to know how to be. I was devastated, but held it in. I wanted to be strong and look after my wife as I knew that she was already heartbroken. Me crying would just add to that pain for her.

This was a mistake. The moment I let my guard down and really showed how I was feeling through being honest, led to one of the best moments of our relationship. We both held each other and felt the pain together. I think it was that moment that a new, unspoken connection and bond between us grew. It is in these difficult, overcast situations that relationships can really develop. For that I am thankful.

My hope is that through reading about my experience it opens the door for other Dads to talk openly. Please share your experiences with me by leaving a comment below. Thanks, Al.

Al and his wife Jen are founders of The Dad Network blog: www.thedadnetwork.co.uk

Fighting Back for our Future: How a Former Boxer Uses His Tough Background to Mentor Boys

By Oliver Wilson

5 Wednesday, January 28, 2009

Golden Gloves Nathan wants to be a champ

By Mark Goode
markgoode@trinitysouth.co.uk

AN UNASSUMING schoolboy is on his way to winning a national title in boxing after his life was turned round by the sport.

Nathan Gray, 13, of Fairfields, Chertsey, won the Southern Counties Champion title at the Amateur Boxing Association's Golden Gloves championship in Southampton last Saturday, in the weight range of 36-38kg.

His mother Caroline said the Jubilee High School student has always wanted to be a boxer after play fighting with his dad from a young age.

She said: "It is a real rags to riches story, because when he started he was a chubby boy and never took his shirt off in front of people.

> **It is a real rags to riches story because when he was a chubby boy"**

"He was told by trainers that he couldn't box unless he lost a stone, so he started doing more exercise and changing his diet and he was allowed in. Now he has got a lot more confidence.

"He is quite reserved anyway and not showy or flashy. He has a heart of gold."

After winning the Southern Counties title last week, Nathan has to win three more heats in order to walk away with the national title later this year for his weight range.

The next round will be in February, in the Midlands.

Caroline said: "He always wanted to box. Even when he was young him and his dad used to box on his bed and Nathan would pretend to cry when he won."

She added he was a normal boy who liked music and football and has trained at Woking Boxing Club since he was 11.

Nathan has been encouraged in his quest by Jubilee High School's motivational officer Oliver Wilson, who also boxes at Woking Boxing Club as well as working at the Addlestone school.

Mr Wilson said: "What I love

about Nathan is that he is so unassuming.

"When you meet him and see him walking around you would-

n't think twice, but he has got such talent. The reason I wanted to help him is because I saw him and he looked like a young me."

GOLDEN BOY: Nathan Gray with school motivational officer Oliver Wilson
Photo C21265-2 by Gray Clark

Coming from a background of eleven children and facing many hardships, I found the motivation and drive to change my life for the better.

On many days my family were faced by the dilemma of heat or eat, and on certain days we did not even have those options.

As my father's alcoholism and gambling became worse I found myself homeless at the age of fourteen. I will never forget the day when my family was faced with eviction from our house, my dad sat at the kitchen table gambling in a card den whilst the bailiffs watched over his shoulder asking him for the outstanding rent, to which he replied "I will give it to you when I have finished this hand."

As fate would have it that was my father's last hand, he lost and the bailiffs removed the chair from under him. The whole family was cast out onto the street and watched as the house was boarded up. It was one of the most painful times I've ever been faced with in my life – where were we going to live and how were we going to survive this predicament?

Our family was ruled by my father's drinking, mood swings, gambling. He always used to threaten us by saying that if we didn't behave ourselves he'd put us in a car and drive us into the Thames.

He would rule the house by having a box of sulphuric acid underneath the sink, and have an axe, where he'd always frighten us by chopping up pieces of furniture in the house, so you can imagine, we didn't ever, ever step out of line.

Impoverished, hungry and violently abused by my father, this resulted in me spending five years in foster care. Food was scarce and it was one of the prime motivators for me to want more!

Although it's not unusual for a poor black boy, born in Britain, to turn to sport; I channelled my energy into boxing and became a boxing champion; I later used this as a stepping stone to succeed beyond the ring.

I created a non-contact boxing motivational program, where men and boys attend, to get fit, get rid of their frustrations, and talk openly about their issues. I assess their problems and direct them to the correct organization to help them.

Through meeting with the young men and boys and relating this story they could feel an empathy with me, as many of them have suffered similar experiences in their lives.

These kids look you in the eye and they know that you're the real deal. They know you've come from, I've come from, where they've come from. And do you know what? My clothes are just a little bit nicer than theirs, that's all.

But they know that with my mentality, my structure, where I want to take them, where I want to go, it's all been structured through discipline. And discipline, explain to the children, is a good thing. Because it gets things done.

In the 21st century we are surrounded by technology and gadgets -- from phones and tablets, to iPods and androids -- while men and boys are being prescribed medication because of the lack of interaction.

Men and boys do cry from the breakdown of family life caused by a myriad of outside influences including gambling, drugs, alcohol and their family's dysfunction.

I believe men and boys need personal connections with positive male role models who can understand where they are coming from.

Are Young Gay Men Burning Up Like Moths?

By Liam Johnson

Just last week I sat with a good friend of mine in a restaurant. Her imminent departure to start a new job in Dubai meant our conversation turned towards futures and growing older.

'How do you feel about getting older?' she asked. 'I never think about gay guys in their 30s and 40s.'

This is something that I had to agree with. I started to think about my peers and how many of them have a detached view of their future.

As a young gay guy growing up in London I can invariably see that the focus of the gay community is on looking good, staying fit and warding off the approaching years. Many gay men I know spend their after work hours pumping away at the gym, their spare time scouring dating sites and their weekends on drug-fuelled binges. It's a huge generalisation of course, but the most prevalent one.

We may have the best hair, the best jobs and the most perfectly Instagrammed smiles but something is missing.

Statistics consistently show that gay men suffer from high rates of depression and anxiety, are more susceptible to recreational drugs and the sexually transmitted diseases that plagued the distant 80s are now becoming a threat once again.

A few weeks ago I was lucky enough to be invited to a summit at King's College in London entitled: 'Does It Really Get Better?' It was a talk between esteemed members of the LGBT community both young and old, discussing what problems each group face.

One speaker, and HIV activist, talked about the worrying rise of HIV infections due to gay men having unprotected sex. By 2012, an estimated 41,000 men who have sex with men were living with HIV in the UK.

I remember one speaker standing up to talk about the issue of loneliness in the gay community. I didn't need a bunch of statistics to tell me that mature gay men report feelings of loneliness.

Books like *The Velvet Rage* by Alan Downs addresses the issue gay men have with growing older. As gay boys we are the sons of heterosexual men. As much we may love and admire our fathers, as I do, we cannot imagine ourselves living the lives as they have done. Settling down, marriage and kids are options that have until recently been ruled out for us and are not paths that seem immediately open to young gay men.

Perhaps it is this fear that drives so many young gay guys to live the outwardly fabulous life of excess, to burn up like moths before their time is over.

I believe gay men need to be taught, from a young age in schools, that the chance of them meeting a solid partner and living a fulfilling live with the possibility of marriage and children is a very real thing. Growing older is not something to fear, rather something to embrace.

If we constantly present young gay men with the idea that life is a quick flash of excess, it will lead them to believe that long and happy lives are still just for straight people. We have a right to future happiness too; we just need to know that it could exist.

Liam is a journalist and freelance writer based in London. You can follow him on Twitter @Liam_JohnsonLDN

It's Great to be A Man

By Theo Merz

When we talk about 'men's issues' there's a natural tendency to focus on the negatives. In my former job as a men's lifestyle writer at the *Daily Telegraph*, I was as guilty of that as anyone: in the past year I've written features on male rape, self-harm among young men, a culture of 'disposable dads', men and depression, men and drug abuse… and others.

Of course, we should be talking about these things. I wouldn't write about them if I didn't believe that, and I'm sure these subjects have been covered in more detail elsewhere in this collection. But if these are the only topics that are covered when men allow ourselves to seriously discuss masculinity, I think we're in danger of losing sight of the bigger picture: that there has never been a better place or time to be a man than here and now.

Personally, I don't buy into the crisis of masculinity narrative that always seems to be brought up when this subject is talked about. Yes, we're in a stage of flux. Yes, some traditional male roles have disappeared and we're not exactly sure how we replace them yet. Yes, the modern male has a whole host of problems that his father and grandfather never had to consider, but he's escaped many more that his father and grandfather never would have been able to.

And that's exactly because we allow ourselves to talk about the sort of subjects I mention above. Whenever I speak to people about male depression and suicide, there's the same reaction. They say it's because men aren't able to talk about their feelings; they say it's because, for men, being men means never showing weakness; they say it's because we're under constant pressure to 'man up' and shy away from contemplating whatever might be bringing us down.

But from what I've seen, this idea of men being out of touch with their emotions is becoming increasingly outdated. I don't just say this from my middle-class, metropolitan bubble. Almost every feature I write, I meet at least one man (usually a young man) who is astonishingly emotionally literate; able to talk about what he's feeling with a candour and precision that his father could never have dreamed of.

Last weekend, for example, I was researching a new programme designed to rehabilitate young offenders. The rehabilitation is based around group therapy and is radically different from what is currently on offer.

Anyway, I spoke with a couple of guys in their early 20s who had been through the course, both of whom had been involved in south London gangs, drugs and one who had been subjected to serious domestic abuse. Neither were ashamed to talk about their past problems and both were very open to alternative versions of masculinity. Neither felt they needed to shut down to the outside world and deny any accusations of weakness to count as a man. It was hard to image them sinking into depression, or at least not because they had no one to talk about their feelings with.

As for me, my friends, my colleagues and the majority of the wide cross-section of men I meet through my work, for them there was no limit to what a man could be. He could be out in the streets of south London, or he could head to the office every day as the main breadwinner for his family, or he could perform as a drag queen in Newcastle every night, or he could lead counselling groups for male victims of domestic abuse. For them, there is no single, set model of masculinity – the idea of which is a little bit terrifying but mostly thrillingly liberating. We get to decide what fills that void.

Perhaps a war or another economic crisis will force us back into more of a set role. For now, though, perhaps we should be grateful for this unprecedented and growing freedom. Everything else aside, I love men and right now I love being one.

Lightning Source UK Ltd.
Milton Keynes UK
UKOW06f1942271015

261485UK00020B/560/P